Whilst It Is Day

Whilst It Is Day

Shedding Light on the Eternal Stakes of Life

*Being an an abridged, popular version of the
doctoral thesis published under the name:
L'option finale dans la mort, Réalité ou mythe?*

❧

DOM PIUS MARY NOONAN OSB

CANA PRESS

Cum permissu Superiorum

For information, address:
PO Box 85
Colebrook,
Tasmania, 7027,
Australia

notredamemonastery.org

ISBN
978-0-6488688-5-9

In memory of my parents, Robert Emmet (1917-1996)
and Marie (Passafiume) Noonan (1924-2011),
who taught me that there is nothing more important in life
than a happy and a holy death.

CONTENTS

FOREWORD

I T IS COMMONPLACE among many Catholics today to see God as a God of love and mercy, who accepts and affirms us no matter what we do. A result of this emphasis is that many now believe that everyone will get to Heaven, despite how they may have lived their lives. This view of God is often contrasted to a supposed pre-Vatican II view of God as a God of judgement and condemnation.

God is a God of love, God is full of mercy, but he is also a God of justice. The Sacred Scriptures clearly teach that when Christ returns in glory he will come "to judge the living and the dead" as declared in the Apostles' Creed. The Lord taught on many occasions that there would be a final judgement at the end of time. The parable of the sheep and goats given in Matthew 25 graphically captures a separation of those destined for beatitude and those destined for damnation.

Each of us must render an account of our lives before the judgement seat of God. Catholic teaching describes a particular judgement at the moment of death. There will be a final judgement at the end of time when the body will be resurrected.

The popular view that nobody is in Hell contradicts both Sacred Scripture and Church teaching, and can lead to a casual approach to addressing the need to strive for one's salvation. As St Paul reminds us, we should work out our salvation in "fear and trembling" (Phil 2:12). It is no trifling matter.

Fr Pius Noonan has offered an excellent reflection on the subject of death and judgement. He was stirred to write this book by the emergence among some theologians of the idea that everyone, at death, will be given the opportunity of taking a final option to choose God. This theory is inconsistent with Catholic teaching, as Fr Noonan clearly shows.

This book is timely and, for this generation, it is a sober reminder of the Church's teaching on the "four last things"—death, judgement, Heaven and Hell. Far from being a morbid view on life the book is, in fact, a lively encouragement to live well that we might die well.

☩ *Julian Porteous*
Archbishop of Hobart

INTRODUCTION

THIS BOOK IS about death, but there is no reason to be afraid, for it is even more about life, the true life we all aspire to. Death is the obligatory gateway into eternity, that blink of an eye through which we pass into another world, a world that is all around us, but which we cannot see with the eyes of our flesh. Some will suggest that in order to best enjoy what life has to offer, one must avoid thoughts of death, and cross that bridge when we get there. It is the intention of this book to show that such is precisely what we must *not* do.

In our day, no stone remains unturned to remove death from our horizon, to pretend that it is nothing, that all that counts is our life in this world. And yet, people continue to die each day. We may wonder if, even from a purely rational point of view, this imposed silence is a good thing. Is it *really* useful to avoid thinking about death? The thought that we must die, does it not allow us to orient ourselves towards living the best life possible? Christianity certainly offers a response to this question by reminding us of the brevity of life and the eternal retribution that awaits us after death. Christian revelation, in effect, speaks to us with the greatest possible clarity of the fact that we die only once and after death we will be judged and receive an unending recompense—blessed or miserable—according to the manner in which we have lived. This great truth is our principal concern in these pages.

Even though this book will offer plenty of food for thought for everyone, it assumes acceptance or at least knowledge of basic Catholic doctrine, and is aimed particularly at two kinds of believers: 1) those who are not concerned about death because, so they think, everybody goes to Heaven, and so there is nothing to worry about; 2) those who believe in eternal life and in judgment after death, but who seek to rest secure in this life by promising themselves an opportunity to settle their accounts with God when they die. For in modern times there are some, probably with the best intentions in the world, who so modify the Christian teaching on death and judgment as to allow everyone to choose his/her own destiny with God *when they are already dead.*

In one of its particular, fairly recent, manifestations, this approach has come to be called the "final option in death", a theory which seeks to establish that each person, at the very moment of his death or immediately thereafter, has the possibility to see God and choose eternal life. In such a way, everyone would have the opportunity to see clearly what is at stake and choose an eternal life of communion with God in the very moment at which one enters eternity.

The spanner in the works is that it is part of Catholic dogma that this life, and *this life alone*, is the stage in which one works out one's salvation. The grace of salvation is offered to all, but when we look at the world, and see that so many apparently live with little concern for eternity, we can be led to fear for the salvation of great numbers of people.

The Church has always encouraged the faithful to prepare for death, and she gives them the support of her prayers and sacraments in the last moments of life; still, many souls die without giving any clear sign of turning to God. Before death, many would seem to be far from God and on the path to damnation. The Church has also repeatedly condemned different forms of a final restoration of all things, usually known as "Origenism", and referring to any number of theories which put forth some kind of final restoration (*apokatastasis* in Greek) by which all human souls and all angels will ultimately be saved. Today one finds reference to the theory of universalism, which, in some respects at least, can be assimilated to Origenism. Contrary to such theories, the Church teaches that there can be no conversion after death.

The proponents of the final option theory thought they could find another way to salvation. Seeing that in many cases there seems to be no conversion before death and admitting that there can be no conversion after death, they suggest that there might be, not before nor after, but *in the very moment of* death a means of meeting God and converting to Him. Such is the reasoning that leads to the final option hypothesis.

Many philosophical and theological subtleties accompanied the elaboration of this hypothesis. We need not be concerned with them here; all has been carefully documented in the doctoral thesis published in 2015 under the French title *L'option finale dans la mort, Réalité ou mythe?*[1] This present work would like to present to the reader in a simple, concise form the essential conclusions of that research.

---

[1] A translation of this thesis is now underway.

When any novel doctrine is taught in the Church, the *sensus fidei*—the "sense of the faith", we would say today the "default position"—must interrogate. Faith is not something to be reinvented in every generation. It was given to us by the Apostles, and even though our understanding of it can and does grow, this progress must always be in the same direction, in fidelity to the same teaching. So the principle question we have to answer is: is this doctrine in conformity with the data of faith? But we will perceive very quickly that this question is actually dependant on another: is it in conformity with sound philosophy? As we go along, we will also see that there is a lot riding on this new reading of death and judgment. The consequences of positing an about face when one has already gone through the gates of death reach far with their implications on the moral life and pastoral approaches. It will be clear that the subject cannot be properly treated without a general survey of its many ramifications.

As, it is hoped, it will become clearer as we proceed, the teaching of Jesus about death and judgment is part of the Gospel, the *euangelion*, the Good News, because it teaches us that we are destined to see God forever if we live in His grace and love, and that it is actually possible to achieve that. We are not doomed to failure in this life; we are not automatons; we do not have to let ourselves be led along by our passions or by the dominant ideology; no, we can, with God's grace, stand up now, today, at this very instant, and live a life that deserves Heaven; we can be virtuous; we can be saints. And if we do, the moment of death will be for us one of immense confidence and peace, for we shall then meet a Judge whom we have loved and served in this life. Such is one of the most fundamental teachings of the Gospel, one that I hope, dear Reader, you will be convinced of as you read these pages.

At the end, may the beauty of the truth shine forth once again and give us renewed incentive to be "co-workers with the truth" (3 Jn 1:8).

I

MY SOUL AND I

FAITH DOES NOT exist in a vacuum. It exists in man.[1] In order to avoid falling into error about the faith, it is very helpful to know what and who man is. Our first considerations will therefore be at the purely human level.

Man is a complex being. His body belongs to the animal world, but his soul is in the realm of spirits. This composite reality has always been the object of the reflections of philosophers. Efforts to explain it go from the evolutionist/materialist thesis—common today—according to which man is nothing more than a highly developed animal, to the one that we could call Platonist/Cartesian, according to which man is essentially a spirit who happens to find itself for a determined amount of time enclosed in an animal body.[2] The former is attractive to the sensual man, for it seems to afford him some justification for his dissoluteness. The latter is also enticing, for at first sight it seems that it elevates the human being, stressing his spiritual essence and inspiring him to not live as an animal. In this sense, we find many Christian authors basing themselves to a

---

[1] The word "man" in these pages is used as being inclusive of male and female, as in Gen. 1:27.

[2] Both Plato and Descartes are famous for having so much insisted on the spiritual nature of man that it is hard to know what role the body plays in human life.

certain extent on this anthropology. But at first sight only. For when we delve deeper, we find such a philosophy of man has a very serious drawback: if man is essentially a soul, it matters little in the end what his body does, for he doesn't really have control over it anyway; what really matters is reaching death, and there, being freed from the body.

There is no need to insist here upon the consequences of such thinking: the essential unity of man is ruined. He is no longer the masterpiece of creation who was meant to dominate with the light of his mind the material world: he becomes a lost atom in a hostile universe, unable to have any influence over matter, and waiting impatiently till that unfortunate union of his body and soul ceases. In the meanwhile, the partisans of both philosophies often find themselves wallowing in the same mire of vice, because, if the flesh is in revolt against the spirit, it can only be tamed if its union with the spirit is one that affects its very essence, that is to say, is constitutive of the being of man. On the contrary, if the union is purely accidental, then it is no surprise that the control of the mind is ever fragile and inadequate.

Neither of the two aforementioned theses, therefore, takes into account the whole of reality: if it is true that man is a sophisticated animal, it is no less true that his capacity to reason places him well beyond the animal world. What's more, if it is true that man is spirit, it is not true in the sense that he would be essentially spirit and his link with the body would be in some way an "accident".

"Man is not his body nor his soul", wrote St Thomas Aquinas in a lapidary statement.[3] The Angelic Doctor was

---

[3] St Thomas Aquinas, *Summa contra Gentiles*, II, 89, trans. James F. Anderson.

able to formulate this teaching thanks to his synthesis of the teaching of Aristotle and the revelation of the New Testament handed down by Tradition. There can be no doubt that this position of St Thomas is among the definitive fundamental elements of Christian anthropology.

King of the visible creation, man enjoys unique power to rule over inferior beings; but he has the duty also to humble himself towards those which surpass him. Man cannot abandon His place in the universe, nor can he change it—his grandeur consists in acknowledging it. The foundation of this grandeur is the fact that he is endowed with intellect and free will. Alone among animals, he can understand the world around him and he can make choices which are not inspired only by physiological needs. This entails an unavoidable consequence: the choices of man engage both his body and his soul. When man decides to do good, he does so in and through his body; when he does evil, he does so in and through his body; this is what we properly call a *human act.*

Let's take an example. The action of nutrition in a man and a horse is materially similar, but formally different: the horse eats by necessity to follow an instinct; it does not deliberate; man, even though he too finds himself in the necessity to eat, gives to the same action a value of a higher order: he chooses what, when and where he will eat, in function of rational or irrational criteria. He can choose sobriety and temperance in eating and drinking in conformity with reason, but he can also choose to eat and drink to excess and pay the consequences. In any case, his behaviour will necessarily be of another order from that of the animal. We can see from this example that it is impossible for a man to abstract from his body and act as if he were an angel; it is also impossible for him to behave in a purely animal way and forget that he is endowed with a spiritual soul.

In other words, body and soul were meant by God to "live together", to support each other. The body of man is perfectly adapted to his soul in such a way that without it, the body dies: a corpse is not a human being. In the same way, the soul without the body is what we call a "separated soul", one which, due to its spirituality and immortality, survives the death of the body, but retains a longing to be reunited with it. In the meantime, it must live without it, in a state which, from the sole point of view of nature, is quite unnatural (*praeter naturam* is St Thomas' technical expression): the soul does not function properly without its body, for it was not meant to. Unlike angels, who are pure spirits and who do not need a body, the human soul derives its knowledge through the senses, and so during the time it is separated from these, it is in an inferior state, even if we know from Divine Revelation that it can make use of its intellectual faculties and be elevated to the vision of God by a very special grace called the "light of glory". The separated human soul alone is not a complete human being.

This is precisely one of the areas in which the hypothesis of the final option in death goes astray. It presumes that man can arrive at the fullness of his being only when his soul is disengaged from his body. This is to make of man an incarnate angel, to posit that only his soul is truly great and has worth before God, that it alone can pronounce itself for the whole, and that, finally, it will be in a better position to choose Him when it will be divested of its body. It is easy to see that the hypothesis in question dissolves man, who is a substantial unity of body and soul. Such thinking, which comes from philosophical idealism with roots in Platonic and Cartesian philosophy, makes light of the body and all things corporeal in the life of man, in sum, his entire earthly existence.

We must add that considering man as an incarnate angel reveals a profound ignorance of the essential difference between human and angelic intellectual activity. St Thomas makes it clear that the act of understanding of a man and that of an angel are not specifically the same, for the angel understands without a reasoning process, whereas the human soul understands discursively, that is to say, humans know causes from their sensible effects, and can come to understand the essences of things only from their sensible accidents.[4] Consequently, it is erroneous to want to allow man's soul to make an option in the angelic way. Under pain of completely distorting human acts themselves, one must avoid assimilating the choices of man and those of the angel. If the angel can, in an instant, perceive all the consequences of his choices and pose once and for all an act which engages him definitively, it is not so for man, who must learn progressively to control his thoughts and master his tendencies. This is so true that St Thomas was able to affirm: "After this life there remains in man no capacity to acquire the ultimate end. The soul needs a body for the obtaining of its end, in so far as it acquires perfection through the body, both in knowledge and in virtue."[5]

A consequence of this is that it is by means of the choice for the ultimate end in this life and by daily putting into practice that choice by the means which lead to it, that man becomes more and more human, more and more free. By confusing the choice of man with that of the angel, on the

---

[4] Cf. St Thomas Aquinas, *The Soul (De Anima)*, q. 7, ad 1.

[5] St Thomas Aquinas, *Summa Contra Gentiles*, III, 144, trans. Vernon J. Bourke.

contrary, the hypothesis of the final option infringes gravely upon human liberty which it fails to understand. According to the final option hypothesis, *man becomes free only when he is no longer a man.*

This also has another grave consequence, namely the suppression of all philosophical and theological discourse on the true nature of human liberty, which must grow and develop throughout life through the repetition of virtuous actions. One of the most decisive consequences of a measured understanding of freedom is that man must cultivate himself and grow in virtue and the practice of good; he must create in himself good habits. This does not just happen; it supposes effort. By means of repeated choices, in harmony with the dignity of his nature, man becomes more and more free with regard to the impulses he shares with the animal world. On the contrary, the man who does not make this effort falls from his human dignity and destroys himself.

Soul and body must live and work and grow together, for "my soul is not I."[6]

---

[6] St Thomas Aquinas, *Commentary on the First Epistle to the Corinthians*, c. 15, no. 924, trans. Fabian Richard Larcher, The Aquinas Institute for the Study of Sacred Doctrine, 2012, vol. 38, p. 349.

2

CROSSING OVER

LIKE EVERY CORPOREAL being, the human being will one day decompose. Death—the separation of the soul (the life principle) from the body which returns to dust—comes to put an end to human existence properly so-called, for alone the composite body/soul constitutes the human person. The soul goes on living, for it is immortal, but its existence separated from the body is an existence in some way incomplete; this is why the soul aspires to the final resurrection. In the meantime, any activity the soul has cannot be, in the strict sense, human activity.

Medicine and science seek to give us a physiological definition of death, the principal signs of which are irreversible cessation of pulmonary and cardiac functions. There are debates surrounding the use of terms, and there is much discussion about "clinical death" as opposed to "biological death". Be that as it may, the irreversible separation of body and soul, which is the real moment of death in the full sense of the term, cannot be detected with certitude by scientific instruments. This is why the greatest precautions should be taken to not pronounce someone dead who is not. Philosophically and theologically speaking, as long as the soul is not separated from the body, the person is not really dead.

The very instant this invisible separation of body and soul takes place, however, is not measurable time; it is the *frontier* between life and death. In other words, either a person is alive or dead; if he is alive, he is not dead; if he is dead, he is not alive; for one cannot be alive and dead at the same time. Here we encounter one of the fallacies upon which the hypothesis of the final option rests, namely that the instant of death is conceived of as being an extensible moment in which the soul could not only become fully conscious of itself but also, in case of need, change its orientation and be converted to God. This is impossible. That is why it is advisable to avoid designating death by means of expressions such as "passage", for the term evokes a time that is more or less long. The physiological process of the decomposition of the body which leads to death can be long; but the precise moment of death is not measurable in time.

As soon as it has left the body, the soul finds itself in what the scholastics called *aevum,* that is to say, the state proper to created spirits. The *aevum* is not eternity in the strict sense, for eternity belongs to God alone who has neither beginning nor ending. The *aevum* is the state in which the soul can no longer modify its fundamental orientation, for it is no longer united to a body.

We can see now, by remaining in the purely philosophical realm, that death is prepared for by a more or less long time during which the soul is united to the body, and that the soul can produce human acts only if the appropriate organs of the body are able to function. Consequently, when it arrives at the moment of death, the soul is henceforth in the *aevum;* the moment of death is the first moment in the *aevum*; it is entirely in the afterlife, and in no way in the present life.[1]

Nevertheless, the hypothesis of the final option would like for there to be in the instant of death, at one and the same time, *an instant without measure and a time which lasts.* The first is required to not fall into the error according to which one can convert after death—the option must imperatively take place in the moment of death. The second is necessary, for without a certain length of time, one cannot conceive how the soul could become conscious of itself and radically change its orientation—death is therefore looked upon as having a measurable length and being instantaneous at the same time, which is a blatant contradiction.

What we refer to as the "moment of death" is in reality the same thing as death itself. In other words, there is no gradual entry into death. It is an instantaneous transformation. Up until a precise moment, the person is alive; from that precise moment on, the person is dead. And once he is dead, he is in a state where all change becomes impossible, for only in the body and through the body, which is the source of all change, can the soul modify itself and its orientations. And so it becomes clear that it is impossible to admit of any final option in death, for the soul will then be deprived of the essential instrument it would need to make a choice, that is, the body.

When one comes to understand these sound, tested principles of anthropology—the soul and the body are naturally

---

[1] The afterlife and the present life are what are called in scholastic terminology the *status termini* —literally, the state of the end of life, and the *status viæ*—literally, the state of being "on the way" to the final end.

intended to be united to each other—there is no difficulty whatsoever in grasping that death, in itself, is necessarily an evil. For Christians, this philosophical fact allows us to understand what gravity of those words God spoke to Adam after forbidding him to eat of the tree of the knowledge of good and evil: *For in what day soever thou shalt eat of it, thou shalt die the death* (Gen 2:17). The terrible punishment of death, presented throughout the Bible as the end of human life, is such that—short of eternal damnation—one cannot possibly imagine anything worse that could happen to a man: it is the end of who he is, the dismembering of his composite being. From faith, we know that we will rise again on the last day, but in the meantime, we must undergo the supreme humiliation of ceasing to be who we are as human beings and accept to live on in an unnatural state until we recover our bodies at the final resurrection at the end of time.

This affirmation, however, does not diminish in any way what we often find in the writings of Christian authors, following St Paul, that the Christian longs to be delivered from his body to go and be with Christ (cf. Phil 1:23). For the hypothesis of the final option, on the contrary, the greatest evil (death) becomes the greatest good. Indeed, if we follow this hypothesis, it is no longer a question, as with St Paul, St Ambrose,[2] or any number of other Christian authors, of the sanctification of death thanks to faith in the death and resurrection of Jesus Christ; it is a question of death itself wrongly perceived as being the climax of natural life, to such an extent that it is not an exaggeration to speak of a veritable docetism[3] of death. It is quite simply impossible, within the

[2] This Father of the Church actually wrote a treatise entitled: *De Bono Mortis, Of the Good of Death.*

[3] Docetism is a heresy according to which the humanity of Christ was a

realms of realistic and human philosophy, for death to be good. God did not intend for us to die. It was not in His plan. He made us for life.

When we cross over, it's over.

---

fiction, an appearance of humanity without any real consistence, whose goal was just to instruct humanity in the ways of God. A "docetism of death" would mean that death does not really affect man. In other words, he would not really be a bodily being at all—his body would not be part of who he is.

3

A LAMP TO MY FEET[1]

I N BOTH THE Old and New Testaments, the course of our earthly life is unique, and after its completion there is no longer any time to change or to merit; rather it is the time to reap the fruits of one's labours.

Already in the Book of Deuteronomy (30:15-19), God had made it clear that in this life we have a choice to make which will have lasting consequences:

> Consider that I have set before thee this day life and good, and on the other hand death and evil, that thou mayst love the Lord thy God, and walk in His ways, and keep His commandments and ceremonies and judgments, and thou mayst live, and He may multiply thee, and bless thee in the land, which thou shalt go in to possess. But if thy heart be turned away, so that thou wilt not hear, and being deceived with error thou adore strange gods, and serve them: I foretell thee this day that thou shalt perish.... I call heaven and earth to witness this day, that I have set before you life and death, blessing and cursing. Choose therefore life, that both thou and thy seed may live.

[1] Cf. Psalm 118:105: "Thy Word is a lamp to my feet".

The Wisdom literature of the Old Testament in general underlines the fact that we must do good in this life, for after death it will be too late: "Do good to thy friend before thou die, and according to thy ability, stretching out thy hand give to the poor" (Sir 14:13); "Delay not to forsake sins, neglect it not till you are in distress. Let nothing prevent the prompt payment of your vows; wait not to fulfil them when you are dying" (Sir 18:21-22 NAB). Another passage teaches us that not only is this life the only one where we can do good, but also that there will be a recompense on the very day of death: "It is easy before God in the day of death to reward every one according to his ways" (Sir 11:28).

The book of Ecclesiastes contains a statement which has played a paramount role in the development of the Church's teaching on death and judgment: "If the tree fall to the south, or to the north, in what place soever it shall fall, there shall it be" (Ecc 11:3). The image, which strikes by its simplicity, of the tree which falls and remains on the side where it was naturally leaning, has inspired an abundant literature and commentary. Already St Jerome had given it an explicit anagogical interpretation.[2] St Thomas for his part quotes this inspired passage frequently. He writes, for example, in the Compendium of Theology:

> The soul will remain perpetually in whatever last end it is found to have set for itself at the time of death, desiring that state as the most suitable, whether it is good or evil. This is the meaning of Ecclesiastes 11:3: "If the tree

[2] See St Jerome, *Commentary on Ecclesiastes*, 11, 3. "Anagogical" means the mystical interpretation of a word or a passage of Scripture which sees in it an allusion to Heaven or life after death.

fall to the south or to the north, in what place soever it shall fall, there shall it be." After this life, therefore, those who are found good at the instant of death will have their wills forever fixed in good. But those who are found evil at that moment will be forever obstinate in evil.[3]

Following St Thomas' lead in this reading of Holy Scripture, a constant interpretation of theologians establishes that death puts a definitive end to the state of probation; after death, one can no longer merit, demerit or convert.

Passing over to the New Testament, we need only to cull a few passages among many. At the beginning of the story of the man born blind, Jesus says to His apostles: "I must work the works of Him that sent me, whilst it is day: the night cometh, when no man can work" (Jn 9:4). Numerous Fathers of the Church and Scripture scholars interpret this verse in the following way: the "day" is the time of our life in this world in which it is given us to work for our salvation and merit eternal life; the "night" is death, after which the time of mercy is over. St John Fisher, in a theological work to refute the errors of Martin Luther, went so far as to say that one would have to be extremely obstinate not to acknowledge this text as affirming that after death it is no longer possible to merit.[4]

In the eschatological discourse presented to us by St Matthew (ch. 24 and 25), after having announced the end of time and the return of the Son of Man, the Lord adds

---

[3] St Thomas Aquinas, *Compendium of theology*, I, 174, trans. Cyril Vollert, Angelico Press, 2012, p. 190.

[4] St John Fisher, *Refutation of M. Luther*, 1524. The reader will have noticed that this text from John 9:4 has inspired the title of our book.

no less than six parables destined to encourage the disciples to make themselves ready: the flood, the thief in the night, the unfaithful servant, the ten virgins, the talents, the last judgment. The leitmotif is clear: the Son of Man will return at an unknown hour, and then we must be ready, for the moment of His coming is no longer the moment to act.

> They knew not till the flood came and took them all away: so also shall the coming of the Son of man be… Watch ye therefore, because you know not what hour your Lord will come. But this know ye, that, if the goodman of the house knew at what hour the thief would come, he would certainly watch and would not suffer his house to be broken open. Wherefore be you also ready, because at what hour you know not, the Son of man will come (Mt 24:39, 42-44).

Why, might we ask, is this so? Why didn't Jesus just tell us the year and day of His return? According to St Gregory the Great, the Lord left the last hour in deep obscurity in order to help men live in the fear of God and be ever prepared.[5] Ignorance of the last hour therefore has a moral goal: to leave all generations, that is to say, every single person, in a certain unsettledness, to arouse them to live according to the Faith, to disengage themselves from material and immediate preoccupations, to fight evil, to suffer for the justice of God's kingdom. This expectation plays the role of leaven which preserves humanity, maintains the ideal of justice and inspires heroic virtues. It is precisely because they are children of light that the faithful should incite themselves to keep

---

[5] Cf. St Gregory the Great, *Homily 13 on the Gospels.*

watch unceasingly, without ever allowing themselves to drift into spiritual indolence. The darkness of death surprises only those who grow numb in sin.[6]

The parable of the ten virgins (Mt 25:1-13) offers a particularly poignant lesson. The essential characters of this parable are the Spouse who arrives when he chooses; the wise virgins who have understood that they must be always ready and who therefore reject every preoccupation that might put them in danger of missing the rendezvous; the foolish virgins who were ready *before* the hour and multiply their efforts *after* the hour, but are not ready at the crucial moment.

In their wait, all the maidens fall asleep, and in the middle of the night, the cry rings out: "Behold the bridegroom cometh. Go ye forth to meet him". So they all rise and trim their lamps. The ones who had made no provisions ask the others to share their oil. These, however, knowing they could not provide both for themselves and the others, refuse. So the foolish virgins have no choice but to go and buy their own. In the meanwhile, the five wise virgins enter the wedding feast, and—the door is closed. Hardly has it been closed, the others return and knock at the door: "Lord, Lord, open to us". But from the inside the bridegroom replies: "Amen, I say to you, I know you not". And the parable concludes: "Watch ye therefore, because you know not the day nor the hour".

The central message of the entire parable is clear: there is only one hour to enter the wedding feast, the hour when the Spouse decides to come. In the same way, there is only one hour to enter into Heaven, and that is the one when

---

[6] Cf. Cornelius a Lapide, *Commentary on Holy Scripture, On S. Matthew*, Vivès, t. 15 (1866) p. 520.

God comes and takes with Him those whom He finds ready at the moment of death. The soul which is not ready at the moment of God's arrival, is not recognised by Him and will miss its destiny. When the hour of death comes, those who have no oil of good works will find no entrance into the eternal wedding feast; all their efforts after death are futile, for this life alone is *our* time, the time to believe, to love, to serve, to act for God and neighbour.

For St Hilary, the great lesson of this parable is that all souls are invited to the eternal nuptials with the heavenly King; for this, it is given to each person to live here below with his mortal body which, like a vessel, must be filled with the oil of good works. Nothing, not even the intercession of the saints, symbolised by the wise virgins, can replace the practice of good works performed in this life: personal merits are not interchangeable, each person is responsible before the Lord for himself.[7] St Augustine expressed the same thought in this lapidary formula: "It is in this life that all the merit or demerit is acquired, which can either relieve or aggravate a man's sufferings after this life. No one, then, need hope that after he is dead he shall obtain merit with God which he has neglected to secure here."[8]

Mention must also be made of the six New Testament passages which, by comparing the Son of Man to a "thief" who arrives at an unknown hour (Mt 24:43; Lk 12:39; 1 Th 5:2; 2 Pt 3:10; Ap 3:3; 16:15), highlight the sudden and unexpected nature of the coming of the Lord. If the thief comes at an unforeseen hour, by means of this comparison the

---

[7] Cf. St Hilary, *Treatise on the Gospel of St Matthew*, ch. 27, n. 5.

[8] Cf. St Augustine, *Enchiridion (Handbook on Faith, Hope and Charity)* ch. 110, trans. J.F. Shaw, Nicene and Post-Nicene Fathers, First Series, Vol. 3. Christian Literature Publishing Co., 1887.

Holy Spirit has willed to make clear that Christ will return suddenly. St Thomas expressed it this way in his commentary on the Creed:

> The judgment ought indeed to be feared… because of the inflexible justice of the Judge. The present is the time for mercy; but the future is the time solely for justice; and so the present is our time, but the future is God's time: "When I shall take a time, I shall judge justices" (Ps 74:3 Vulgate). "The jealousy and rage of the husband will not spare in the day of revenge. Nor will he yield to any man's prayers; nor will he accept for satisfaction ever so many gifts"(Prov 6:34-35).[9]

This time of God (*tempus Dei*) to which Aquinas refers here has a profound meaning; the time of man goes up until death; after death, it is God who separates the just from the wicked. Until death, men make their decisions; after death, God decides for them, that is to say, He sanctions the decisions they made during their lifetime: "He shall separate them one from another, as the shepherd separateth the sheep from the goats" (Mt 25:32). Clearly, the insistence here on the verb "to separate" shows that, at the time of the final judgment, each person will no longer have the capacity to choose his place. The place will be assigned to him by the King; the time for human choices will have passed.

A number of other passages insist upon the connection between what happens *now* and what will happen *then*, to highlight the difference between what occurs in this life and

---

[9] Cf. St Thomas Aquinas, *Commentary on the Creed*, a. 7, trans. Joseph B. Collins.

what will eventuate after death. Far from being the simple continuation of earthly life, life after death presents itself as the time of retribution, as is clearly expressed in the beatitudes according to St Luke, with the quadruple comparison: now you are hungry, then you will be filled… now you are rich, then you will be poor, etc. (cf. Lk 6:21-25), which gives us to understand that there is no intermediary time or state through which one can pass from one side to the other: the present state determines the definitive destination.

In the Gospel according to St John, Jesus also establishes an antinomy between this world and the life to come. If one wants to preserve life in the *other* world, one must hate it in *this* world: "He that loveth his life shall lose it and he that hateth his life in this world keepeth it unto life eternal" (Jn 12:25). The conclusion is unavoidable: there can be no question of preserving life (understand *the life of grace*) after death if, in this world, one has not mortified—the verb "hate" is intentionally used to stress the energy required to master one's passions—his own will in order to embrace the Divine Will.

This lesson is strongly urged by Jesus in the parable of the wheat and the cockle, of which He Himself has given us the exegesis: the good sower is the Son of Man, the good seed the children of the kingdom, the cockle weeds are the children of the devil who sowed them in the good field, the harvest is the end of the world, the harvesters are angels—and significantly here for our purposes: "The field is the world" (Mt 13:38). The field is *this world, not the afterlife*. This word "field" is reminiscent of, say, a football field. As long as the players (and the ball) are on the field, they can score goals, but if they leave the field, they are disqualified from the game. So it is with this all-important event which is our life, and which

St Paul compares to a sporting event: "Know you not that they that run in the race, all run indeed, but one receiveth the prize. So run that you may obtain" (1 Cor 9:24). In other words, we have all the time of this life to choose God and live according to His commandments, but when the hour of death comes, the game is over. If the field in which the eschatological realities are prepared is this world, that can only mean that it is in *this* world, in this world *only*, that the eternal destiny of each human being is decided. There is no other field, there is no other threshing floor, there is only this world as we know it, in which God sows His good grain and the devil sows his cockle. Both grow until the harvest at the end of the world, the end of time.

In his Second Epistle to the Corinthians, St Paul writes words which are probably the most important of all those we have already cited. He affirms: "For we must all appear before the judgment seat of Christ, so that each one may receive recompense, according to what he did in the body, whether good or evil" (2 Cor 5:10, NAB). It follows from this text that, not only must each of us pass before the tribunal of Christ to receive our reward, but this reward will depend upon what we will have done while *in the body;* consequently, the judgment is in relation with what was done during the terrestrial situation, not in any supposed passage between life and death. The apostolic doctrine establishes with clarity that our eternal destiny depends strictly upon our behaviour in this world. "Whilst we have time, let us work good to all men" (Gal 6:10) — "whilst we have the time", that is to say, here, now, in this life. The author of the Epistle to the Hebrews puts it succinctly: "It is appointed unto men once to die, and after this the judgment" (Hb 9:27).

Finally the book of Apocalypse (20:12) tells us:

> I saw the dead, great and small, standing in the presence of the throne. And the books were opened: and another book was opened, which was the book of life. And the dead were judged by those things which were written in the books, according to their works.

All our thoughts, words and deeds are written on those scrolls, all is recorded. When we die, the scroll is read and we are judged according to what is written.

> *Liber scriptus proferetur*
> *in quo totum continetur,*
> *unde mundus iudicetur.*

> *Lo! the book exactly worded,*
> *Wherein all hath been recorded;*
> *Thence shall judgment be awarded.*[10]

All these texts establish that conversion is possible up until death, and this is the sign of great mercy on God's part, for He never closes the door to the sinner who comes back to Him as long as he lives. If this is the case, what possibility of a return or conversion remains, once the soul will have left the field of this world? There is no allusion, either direct or indirect, to such a possibility. Consequently, it would be more than foolish, it would be insane, to count on it.

---

[10] Sequence *Dies irae* from the Requiem Mass for the Dead in the traditional Roman Missal.

God's word is a lamp for our feet, and light for our path.

Let us open our eyes to the divine light, and let us hear with attentive ears the warning that the divine voice crieth daily to us: "Today if ye will hear His voice, harden not your hearts" (Ps 94).[11]

---

[11] St Benedict of Nursia, *Rule*, Prologue.

4

IN MEDIO ECCLESIÆ[1]

I N THE APOSTLES' Creed we profess: "He will come to judge
the living and the dead". Even though the majority of
New Testament texts about the judgment refer explicitly to
the general judgment at the end of time when all of humanity will be gathered together in one place and where each of
us will be publicly judged, there are a number of passages
which refer to a judgment that takes place at the moment
of death. The immediate retribution of souls after death
was clearly referred to by the Lord Himself in at least two
parables relayed to us by St Luke. In chapter 12, replying to
a man who asked him to judge between him and his brother,
Jesus tells a parable which stresses a type of judgment quite
different from the one He is being asked to give. He speaks
of a rich man who, blessed with an abundant harvest, invests
in building bigger barns to store up all his grain, so that he
could sit back, relax and enjoy life for many years. The parable concludes with Jesus saying: "Thou fool, this night thy
life will be demanded of thee" (Lk 12:20). The other parable
in chapter 16 is that of the rich man and poor Lazarus who,
every day, lay at the foot of the rich man's table without
receiving any food. When he dies he is carried by the angels

---

[1] "In the midst of the Church", cf. Sir. 15:5

into the bosom of Abraham, whereas the rich man is buried
in Hell—note once again the passive verbs in both cases:
the poor man *is carried* to Heaven, the rich man *is buried*
in Hell, giving us to understand that they could no longer
make decisions for themselves, but also that the retribution
was immediate, and did not wait till the end of time.

In addition to the story of the poor man Lazarus in Luke
16 and the quotation from Hebrews 9:27 mentioned earlier, there are a few other texts that refer to an immediate
recompense after death, as opposed to waiting till the end
of time and the final judgment. For example, there is the
word of Our Lord to the Good Thief on the cross: "This
day thou shalt be with me in paradise" (Lk 23:43); in other
words, you will not have to wait till the general judgment.
We might also mention the profession of faith of St Paul to
the Corinthians: "For we know, if our earthly house of this
habitation be dissolved, that we have a building of God, a
house not made with hands, eternal in Heaven" (2 Cor 5:1);
and again, in the book of Apocalypse, we read:

> "I heard a voice from Heaven, saying to me:
> Write: Blessed are the dead who die in the Lord.
> From henceforth now, saith the Spirit, that they
> may rest from their labours. For their works follow
> them" (Ap 14:13).

All these point to a reward that follows death without
delay; they therefore implicitly affirm that, long before the
final judgment of the living and the dead at the end of human history, each human being is personally judged at the
moment of death and receives his recompense.

Following the constant teaching of the Church Fathers, St Thomas Aquinas was able to affirm as definitive Church doctrine that death is the end of the time of merit, and that the particular judgment follows immediately after death. Aquinas qualifies as heretical the affirmation that souls must wait till the end of time before they are judged. Basing himself on the parable of Lazarus and the rich man in Luke 16 and on 1 Th 5:2 ("the day of the Lord will come like a thief in the night"), he affirms without hesitation that judgment is passed on each person *in* his death (*in morte ipsius*).[2]

During the lifetime of the Angelic Doctor, we find in the writings of Pope Innocent IV a clear formulation of the eternal punishment of those who die in the state of mortal sin: "If anyone dies unrepentant in a state of mortal sin, there is no doubt but that he will be tormented forever in the fires of eternal Hell."[3] The Second Council of Lyons, which St Thomas would have attended if he had not died on the way, was able to give a concise formulation concerning the immediate retribution of souls, formulation that will be repeated in numerous magisterial documents: "For souls who die in a state of mortal sin or with only original sin, they descend immediately into Hell, where, however, they receive unequal punishments."[4]

Nevertheless, we would have to await the fourteenth century to have a dogmatic definition of the immediate recompense of the just and the chastisement of the damned

---

[2] Cf. S. Thomas Aquinas, *Commentary on the First Epistle to the Corinthians*, ch. 3.

[3] Innocent IV, *Letter to the bishop of Tusculum*, 6 March 1254.

[4] Council of Lyons II, *Profession of faith of the Emperor Michael Paleologos to Pope Gregory X*, 6 July 1274.

after death. Pope John XXII (1316-1334) upheld during a sermon in Avignon on All Saint's Day 1331, that the souls of the
saints will not see God face to face until after the resurrection of the body and the general judgment at the end of time.
Until then, he affirmed, they see the humanity of Christ, but
do not have the beatific vision. The Pope repeated this in
two other sermons that caused scandal. Two cardinals, the
Dominican Durand de Saint-Pourçain and the Cistercian
Jacques Fournier respectfully informed the Pope of their
disagreement and encouraged him to take counsel and declare that he had spoken only as a private theologian. Pope
John XXII humbly followed this advice. The day before his
death, he retracted his teaching and affirmed on 3 December
1334 : "The just souls separated from their bodies and fully
purified are in the Kingdom of Heaven, Paradise (…) They
see God and the Divine Essence face to face". His successor,
Benedict XII, lost not time in putting this controversy to
rest by defining this point of Catholic dogma for all times:

> According to the general disposition of God, the
> souls of all the saints … immediately (*mox*) after
> death and, in the case of those in need of purifica-
> tion, after the purification…, already before they
> take up their bodies again and before the general
> judgment, have been, are and will be with Christ
> in Heaven, in the heavenly kingdom and paradise,
> joined to the company of the holy angels…. More-
> over according to the general disposition of God,
> the souls of those who die in actual mortal sin go
> down into Hell immediately (*mox*) after death and
> there suffer the pain of Hell. Nevertheless, on the
> day of judgment all men will appear with their bod-

ies "before the judgment seat of Christ" to give an account of their personal deeds, "so that each one may receive good or evil, according to what he has done in the body" (2 Cor. 5:10).[5]

This teaching would be repeated by the Council of Florence:

> The souls of those, who after the reception of baptism, have incurred no stain of sin at all, and also those who, after the contraction of the stain of sin whether in their bodies or when released from the same bodies, as we have said before, are purged, are immediately received into Heaven, and see clearly the one and triune God Himself just as He is, yet according to the diversity of merits, one more perfectly than another. Moreover, the souls of those who depart in actual mortal sin or in original sin only, descend immediately into Hell but to undergo punishments of different kinds.[6]

Eternal retribution is therefore made immediately after death. Since there can be no retribution without previous judgment of merits and demerits, this judgment must necessarily take place between death and the retribution. Therefore one must conclude that the particular judgment coincides with the moment of death, which leaves no place for an "option" other than the one already taken before death.

---

[5] Benedict XII, Bull *Benedictus Deus*, 29 January 1336.
[6] Council of Florence, *Decree for the Greeks, Laetentur coeli*, 6 July 1439.

Following the Council of Trent, the Roman Catechism explicitly teaches that the particular judgment "takes place when each one of us departs this life; for then he is instantly placed before the judgment-seat of God, where all that he has ever done or spoken or thought during life shall be subjected to the most rigid scrutiny."[7] The doctrine of the particular judgment at the moment of death is part and parcel of Catholic doctrine.

St Robert Bellarmine, doctor of the Church, affirms that the reality of the particular judgment is sufficiently demonstrated by the word of Sirach that was quoted earlier: "It is easy before God in the day of death to reward every one according to his ways" (Sir 11:28), and the parable of the rich man and Lazarus (Lk 16) which underlines that the damned descend to eternal punishment immediately after death; in the same way, the elect are received immediately into paradise, according to the word of the Lord to the good thief: "This day thou shalt be with me in paradise" (Lk 23:43). For Bellarmine, it is neither credible nor possible that pain and reward should be meted out without a previous judgment.[8] Therefore, the particular judgment takes place at the very moment of death.

Another doctor of the Church, St Francis de Sales, wrote around the same time that after this mortal life there are punishments to be feared, prepared for those who offend the Divine Majesty and die without being reconciled to Him. He teaches clearly that "at the hour of death the soul shall be judged by a particular judgment; and that at the end of the world all shall rise and appear together to be judged again in the universal judgment."[9]

---

[7] *Catechism of the Council of Trent*, Part I, art. 7.

[8] Cf. St Robert Bellarmine, *On Purgatory*, II, 4.

[9] St Francis de Sales, *Treatise on the Love of God*, XI, 18.

In the 19th century, when the First Vatican Council was convoked, a number of schemas had been prepared for discussion, most of which were never opened due to the hasty dispersion of the Council when the Pontifical States were invaded. Even though these texts do not have magisterial authority, they are nevertheless witnesses to the faith of the Church and to what, at the time, was considered to be definable dogma. One of them refers to 2 Cor 5:10 and affirms that after death it is no longer possible to do penance and atone for grave sins, for judgment follows immediately upon death.

So it was that at the beginning of the 20th century, the great Jesuit theologian and Cardinal, Louis Billot, was able to affirm that, in the absence of a solemn definition, one can certify that the Church Fathers and Doctors, when they do not explicitly preach, at least openly suppose it to be a dogma of the Catholic faith that each soul is definitively judged when it leaves this life. For Billot, it cannot be denied that the preparatory way to the future life is completed with death; nor that upon the result of our earthly pilgrimage depends our state of immobility in either salvation or damnation.[10] We may therefore refer to the doctrine which affirms that the particular judgment follows immediately after death as "proxima fidei."[11]

This doctrine is presupposed also by the writings and homilies of the Popes. A good example would be the follow-

---

[10] Cf. L. Billot, *De novissimis*, q. 1, thes. 1, § 1.

[11] "Proxima fidei", literally, "proximate to the faith": this doctrinal note is used to refer to truths which are admitted by the entire Church and for which all that is lacking to make them a dogma of faith is the formal definition made by an ecumenical council or the Pope. For example, the doctrine of the Immaculate Conception of Mary was "proximate to the faith" before the solemn definition made by Blessed Pope Pius IX in 1854.

ing prayer for a happy death, approved by Pope Pius XI, and therefore pertaining to the ordinary pontifical magisterium:

> Let us recall our final end. At every moment I can die and enter into my eternity. In death I will be judged according to my works. If I die in a state of serious sin, I will be eternally miserable with the demons and damned souls in Hell. If I die in the state of grace, I will be forever happy with the angels and the saints in Heaven. My God, grant me the grace to live and die in Thy holy love without ever offending Thee.[12]

The Second Vatican Council summarised this doctrine in a famous passage:

> Since we know neither the day nor the hour, we should follow the advice of the Lord and watch constantly so that, when the single course of our earthly life is completed, we may merit to enter with him into the marriage feast and be numbered among the blessed, and not, like the wicked and slothful servants, be ordered to depart into the eternal fire, into the outer darkness where "men will weep and gnash their teeth."[13]

The pertinence of this text appears most vividly when we realise that the Council here applies to the moment of death the eschatological warnings of Scripture that refer to the end of times.

---

[12] Pius XI, *Explorata res*, AAS XV (1923) 107.
[13] Vatican Council II, *Lumen Gentium*, 48.

In passing, we might draw attention to the fact that at Vatican II, when some of the Council Fathers asked that the dogmatic constitution on the Church be amended to state explicitly that there will actually be people who are damned forever in Hell, the theological commission answered that the text already cites the Gospel which expresses itself, not in the grammatical *conditional*, but in the grammatical *future*; in plain English this means that Jesus is speaking, not of something that *might* happen, but of something that *will* happen; in other words, it was obvious for the Fathers of the Second Vatican Council—so obvious that there was no need to restate it—that there are souls who do go to Hell forever.

This doctrine is repeated and summarised in a complete way by the *Catechism of the Catholic Church*, which is without a doubt the most explicit teaching the Church has ever formulated on these questions. This text deserves particular attention, due to the fact that at the time of its publication by St John Paul II, it was declared "certain" (*tutus*) for the teaching of the Catholic faith.[14]

> Death is the end of man's earthly pilgrimage, of the time of grace and mercy which God offers him so as to work out his earthly life in keeping with the divine plan, and to decide his ultimate destiny... The Church encourages us to prepare ourselves for the hour of our death... Death puts an end to human life as the time open to either accepting or rejecting the divine grace manifested in Christ. The New Testament speaks of judgment primarily in its aspect of

[14] St John Paul II, Apostolic Constitution *Fidei depositum*, 11 October 1992.

the final encounter with Christ in His second coming,
but also repeatedly affirms that each will be rewarded
immediately after death in accordance with his works
and faith. The parable of the poor man Lazarus and
the words of Christ on the cross to the good thief, as
well as other New Testament texts speak of a final
destiny of the soul—a destiny which can be different
for some and for others. Each man receives his eternal
retribution in his immortal soul at the very moment
of his death, in a particular judgment that refers his
life to Christ: either entrance into the blessedness of
Heaven—through a purification or immediately,—or
immediate and everlasting damnation.[15]

This text contains a number of remarkably clear teachings. It affirms, first of all, that death puts an end to man's
pilgrimage on earth, and it specifies that this time, which
is that of grace and the mercy of God, decides the everlasting destiny. It is the time which is opened to this grace, for
earthly life alone can decide on its acceptance or refusal. The
Catechism also mentions retribution as being in function of
faith and works in this life, and refers explicitly to the poor
man Lazarus, a text whose decisive influence on the doctrine
of the particular judgment we have seen. Perhaps even more
important for us is that the retribution is made *immediately
after* death, or rather *at the very moment of death* (*inde a morte
sua*, says the Latin text), which would indicate that there is
no difference between the moment of death and after death.

Before concluding this chapter, it may be useful to evoke,
in addition to this authorised witness of the papal magis-

---

[15] *Catechism of the Catholic Church*, 1013-1014, 1021-1022.

terium, a couple of texts from other approved catechisms which are in favour of the same teaching, and which are proof of a consensus in the universal Church concerning this all-important reality. In *The Teaching of Christ, A Catholic Catechism for Adults*, we read:

> Implicit in the defined teaching of the Church is the teaching that the death of an individual marks the end of his period of trial. For he is then no longer a pilgrim, and no more will he sin or earn merit. God's judgment comes upon him…. Each individual is at the moment of his death all that he has made himself to be by his free acceptance or free rejection of the divine call and gifts… God's judgment clearly indicates to the individual what he has made himself to be, and it gives him the place for which he has fitted himself. In the light of divine judgment the individual recognizes and affirms what he has merited and has become.[16]

Fr John Hardon, in his *The Catholic Catechism*, writes:

> The New Testament is so clear on the subject of death and its aftermath that the Gospels are almost thematic on the need for serving God faithfully in this life, because after death there is no chance of repentance. Christ's parable about Lazarus is unmistakable… St Paul merely confirmed what Christ had

---

[16] *The Teaching of Christ, A Catholic Catechism for Adults*, Ed. By R. Lawler, O.F.M.Cap, D. Wuerl, and T. C. Lawler, OSV, Huntington, Indiana, 1976, pp. 525-527. This catechism bears the imprimatur of Bishop Leo Pursley of Fort Wayne-South Bend.

taught. He spoke of our pilgrimage away from the
Lord as long as we are in the body. Once the body
is shed, we are able to possess the Lord.[17]

Throughout these various formulations, we find the same
doctrine: death marks the end of life here below—the *status
viae*—, and immediately after death, the soul is judged according to what it has made itself to be during its time on earth.
In none of these texts is there any allusion whatsoever to a
moment of choice, option or decision.

In the midst of the Church—*in medio Ecclesiae*—God's
wisdom and truth is made manifest to us. Let us take it to heart,
so that we too may be filled *sapientiae et intellectus*—with
wisdom and understanding.

---

[17] John A. Hardon, S.J., *The Catholic Catechism*, Geoffrey Chapman
1975, pp. 255-256. This Catechism bears the imprimatur of the Vicar
General of New York.

5

GATHER TOGETHER
HIS SAINTS[1]

THE TEACHING OF the Scriptures, authoritatively inter-
preted by the Church, is clear, and leaves no room for
doubt or hesitation; the Scriptures are normative for our
faith. "Mercy and truth have met each other: justice and
peace have kissed", the Psalm teaches us (Ps 84:11), for this
life is given us as a time of mercy, before the hour of definitive justice which immediately follows death. This is good to
keep in mind in the face of a certain tendency to quote only
those passages of Scripture that refer to mercy, forgetting
that there is and will always be divine justice which will exert
itself inexorably in the world to come.

The saints, who read the Scriptures in their entirety and
lived them out in practice, know how to draw out the lessons
in order to lead an upright life to eternal salvation. It would
require volumes to convey all that the saints have written
and preached on this all-important subject. Just a few examples will suffice to give the tenor of their thought. They
are God's friends, and with them we are in good company.

A famous homily of the second century, which was for
a long time attributed to Pope St Clement, illustrates the

---

[1] Cf. Psalm 49:5.

necessity to take advantage of the time of this life in order
to do penance and merit eternal life:

> As long, therefore, as we are upon earth, let us prac-
> tise repentance, for we are as clay in the hand of the
> artificer. For as the potter, if he make a vessel, and it be
> distorted or broken in his hands, fashions it over again;
> but if he have before this cast it into the furnace of fire,
> can no longer find any help for it: so let us also, while
> we are in this world, repent with our whole heart of the
> evil deeds we have done in the flesh, that we may be
> saved by the Lord, while we have yet an opportunity
> of repentance. For after we have gone out of the world,
> no further power of confessing or repenting will there
> belong to us. Wherefore, brethren, by doing the will of
> the Father, and keeping the flesh holy, and observing the
> commandments of the Lord, we shall obtain eternal life.[2]

St Augustine draws a poignant lesson from two of the
Gospel texts we have already alluded to:

> Let man, then, work while he lives, that he may not
> be overtaken by that night when no man can work (cf. Jn
> 9:4). It is now that faith is working by love (cf. Gal 5:6);
> and if now we are working, then this is the day—Christ
> is here... While you live, be doing, if you are to be
> doing at all; for then shall come that appalling night,
> to envelope the wicked in its folds. But even now every
> unbeliever, when he dies, is received within that night:

[2] Pseudo-Clement, *(IIa Clementis) to the Corinthians*, ch. 8. Trans. John
Keith. From Ante-Nicene Fathers, Vol. 9, Christian Literature Publishing Co., 1896.

there is no work to be done there. In that night was the rich man burning, and asking a drop of water from the beggar's finger; he mourned, agonised, confessed, but no relief was vouchsafed. He even endeavoured to do good; for he said to Abraham, "Father Abraham, send Lazarus to my brethren, that he may tell them what is being done here, lest they also come into this place of torment" (Lk 16:24-28). Unhappy man! When you were living, then was the time for working: now you are already in the night, in which no man can work.[3]

Is this not the meaning of these lines of the Patriarch of Western Monks, St Benedict of Nursia, who encourages his monks to fight to win the Kingdom of Heaven:

> Our hearts and bodies must be made ready to fight under the holy obedience of His commands.... And if we would escape the pains of Hell and reach eternal life, then must we—while there is still time, while we are in this body and can fulfil all these things by the light of this life—hasten to do now what may profit us for eternity.[4]

"While we are in the body," insists St Benedict. In the chapter on humility in his Rule, the saint insists on this in a most eloquent manner when he refers to the degrees of humility, comparing them to the rungs of a ladder. The sides of the ladder, he says, are our body and soul.[5] Clearly for the

---

[3] St Augustine, *Tractates on the Gospel of St John*, 44, 6. Trans. John Gibb, from Nicene and Post-Nicene Fathers, First Series, Vol. 7, Christian Literature Publishing Co., 1888.
[4] St Benedict of Nursia, *Rule for Monks*, Prologue, trans. Justin McCann.
[5] Cf. St Benedict of Nursia, *Rule for Monks*, ch. 7.

Father of Western Monasticism, either we go to God with our body and soul together, or we do not go at all. It would take us too far from our topic to develop this thought here; suffice to say that it is hardly conceivable to come up with a more stimulating thought for an ardent spiritual life which spills over into intense activity for the beauty, the harmony and the splendour of life in this world. The countless amazing monuments of monastic architecture and the numerous inventions we are still benefitting from today are there to bear witness to this truth which is obvious to anyone who takes the time to study and admire them.[6]

Among St Benedict's masters, we must count St Basil who writes:

> Let us not remain careless in our laxity; let us not lose the time by continual sloth, always lightly putting off till tomorrow or even later, the beginning of action. Let us fear that one day the One who has redeemed us come to surprise us deprived of good works and reject us from the joys of the nuptial feast. When it will no longer serve any purpose to repent, we will weep in vain and we will regret uselessly the badly used time of our life: "Now is the acceptable time, now is the day of salvation", the apostle tells us (2 Cor 6:2). Now is the time of penance, later will be that of reward; the present is the time of work and labour, the future of recompense; this is the time of suffering, that of consolation. At this moment God comes to the help of those who turn away from wicked paths; later He will be the infallible and formi-

---

[6] For an excellent, easy to read study of the contribution of monks to the development of culture, see Thomas E. Woods Jr., *How the Catholic Church Built Western Civilisation*, Regnery 2005.

dable inquisitor of the actions, words and thoughts of men. Today we can turn His longanimity to our advantage, but we will come to know the justice of His judgments when, at the resurrection of the dead, each of us will receive the recompense for our works, some for chastisement, others for eternal life.[7]

Venerable Louis of Granada, one of the most renowned preachers of 16th century Spain, had this to say about those who defer looking after their souls for some later, uncertain date:

> Some defer this important affair of salvation to an indefinite future; others till the hour of death. Many allege that it is too difficult and arduous an undertaking. Many presume upon God's mercy, persuading themselves that they can be saved by faith and hope without charity. Others, in fine, who are enslaved by the pleasures of the world, are unwilling to sacrifice them for the happiness which God promises. These are the snares most frequently employed by Satan to allure men to sin, and to keep them in its bondage until death surprises them... It will not be difficult to prove that this is a ruse of the father of lies, whose office since the beginning of the world has been to deceive man. We know with certainty that there is nothing which a Christian should desire more earnestly than salvation. It is equally certain that to obtain it the sinner must change his life, since there is no other possible means of salvation.[8]

---

[7] St Basil of Caesarea, *The Monastic Rules,* Prologue, PG 31, 889-892, personal translation.

[8] Venerable Louis of Granada, *The Sinner's Guide*, ch. 24.

Such are the attitudes of the saints.

St John Henry Newman, for his part, expresses dismay in his unequalled prose, concerning those who reassure themselves that they will always have the time for a "quick-fix" conversion from a life of sin:

> In putting off the day of repentance, these men are reserving for a few chance years, when strength and vigour are gone, that work for which a *whole* life would not be enough. That work is great and arduous beyond expression. There is much of sin remaining even in the best of men, and "if the righteous scarcely be saved, where shall the ungodly and the sinner appear?" (1 Pt 4:18). Their doom may be fixed any moment; and though this thought should not make a man despair today, yet it should ever make him tremble for tomorrow.[9]

Closer to us, Pope St John Paul II stressed the link between preparing for death and judgment and living a truly upright moral life. In his apostolic exhortation *Reconcilatio et Poenitentia*, he wrote words whose exceptional force has hardly been noticed, but which need to be repeated today loud and clear:

> The Church cannot omit, without serious mutilation of her essential message, a *constant catechesis* on what the traditional Christian language calls the four last things of man: death, judgment (universal and particular), Hell and Heaven. In a culture which tends to imprison man in

---

[9] St John Henry Newman, *Parochial Sermon 1*, "Holiness Necessary for Future Blessedness".

the earthly life at which he is more or less successful, the pastors of the Church are asked to provide a catechesis which will reveal and illustrate with the certainties of faith what comes after the present life: beyond the mysterious gates of death, an eternity of joy in communion with God or the punishment of separation from him. *Only* in this eschatological vision can one realise the exact nature of sin and *feel decisively moved* to penance and reconciliation.[10]

It is not difficult to understand what the saintly Pope was trying to get across in this essential passage: if a complete eschatological teaching (on death, judgment, Heaven and Hell) is not presented in a consistent manner ("constant catechesis") to the faithful, it is not possible for them to realise the exact nature of sin and be moved effectively to conversion. Let's say that again: if the ultimate truths, our ultimate destiny, and the real possibility of damnation are not heard *often*, one cannot be moved to turn to God. Those words should haunt every single priest who never preaches about eternity and what is at stake in this short life. If we add to these words, Venerable Pius XII's affirmation that "the sin of this century is the loss of the sense of sin,"[11] it becomes easy to understand why the hypothesis of the final option was able to arouse such interest in an age given over to hedonism: along with other false and deadly theories that are based, not on God's revelation, but on man's cowardly efforts to shirk responsibility and find an easy way to Heaven, it leaves one

---

[10] St John Paul II, *Reconciliatio et Poenitentia,* 2 December 1984, no. 26, emphases added.

[11] Venerable Pius XII, *Radio-message to the US National Congress in Boston*, 26 October, 1946. The text was quoted by John Paul II in the exhortation *Reconciliatio et Poenitentia*, 18.

under the illusion that one can live in practice outside of the divine law and be saved in the end when it is all over—like scoring a goal after the final whistle has blown.

In this same line of thought, Pope St Paul VI also had some austere words which should arouse every soul from its spiritual torpor:

> Of the Gospel, one ends up accepting only what has immediate, temporal usefulness for the earthly interests of humanity... All that can be said about Heaven and Hell, one no longer listens to. What becomes, what could become of the world, without this consciousness of the obligation to refer to a transcendent and inexorable justice (cf. Mat 25)? One of the fundamental principles of the Christian life is that it must be lived out in function of its future and eternal eschatological destiny. Yes, it should make us tremble... : *Work out your salvation with fear and trembling* (Ph 2:12). The gravity and incertitude of our final destiny has always been an abundant object of meditation and a source of unparalleled energy for the morals but also for the holiness of Christian life.[12]

It should now be clear that the saints received, lived and preached the Word of God. Let us gather together and offer sacrifice with them. Their doctrine is firm, their way is sure. *Ipsam sequens, non devias - following them, we will not go astray.*[13]

---

[12] St Paul VI, *General Audience*, 28 April, 1971.

[13] This last quotation is from St Bernard of Claivaux's famous homily on the Annunciation (*Super Missus Est*, Sermon 2). The text is applied to Our Lady, but *mutatis mutandis* applies to any saint who shows us the way to God.

6

GOD'S FOOTPRINTS

THE FAITH OF the Church constitutes a majestic edifice whose parts hold each other together in unity. By rejecting or distorting one of these truths, the others are by the very fact threatened. This is particularly so when it comes to eschatology, the teaching on the last end of man. If the hypothesis of the final option were to be accepted, that is, if death is no longer the moment of judgment, and if one can turn to God when one has entered into death, the entire edifice of Catholic dogma collapses.

Faith, the first of the theological virtues, the "foundation and the root of all justification" according to the Council of Trent, is the virtue by which we believe to be true all that God has revealed, for the simple reason that He has revealed it and He cannot be deceived. Without faith, "there has never been justification for anyone."[1] Indeed, for "without faith it is impossible to please God. For he that cometh to God must believe that He is: and is a rewarder to them that seek Him" (Heb 11:6). The *Catechism of the Catholic Church* summarises it this way:

Believing in Jesus Christ and in the One who sent him for our salvation is necessary for obtaining that salvation.

---

[1] Council of Trent, *Decree on justification*, c. 7.

Since "without faith it is impossible to please [God]" and
to attain to the fellowship of his sons, therefore without
faith no one has ever attained justification, nor will anyone obtain eternal life "but he who endures to the end."[2]

Faith is a gift of God, which completely transforms one's
perspective on life, for it opens up undreamed of vistas for
the true meaning of life and eternity. This virtue is infused
by God at baptism and, in the case of infants, the seed which
is then planted in the soul is nurtured and developed by the
study of faith when they arrive at the age of reason. If we
take the case of an adult who discovers the faith, it might
happen something like this. The person would, through
the light of natural reason, come to the conclusion that it is
quite reasonable to believe in God, for the universe cannot
possibly be its own cause. This conviction might lead him
to seek to discover who this God is and if He has revealed
anything about Himself. It is to be hoped that such a person
would hear about Jesus Christ and read the Gospels, there
being confronted with the divinity of Christ and the proof
He gave of His divine mission. The next step would be a
speculative judgment on the possibility and the obligation
to believe, for if God has infallibly revealed some truths, we
are bound to give our assent to them; the will would then
intervene to command the assent of the intellect. Finally, the
theological virtue of faith is infused into the soul by God.

Now, even though the infusion of the gift of faith takes
no time, we can reasonably hold that in most cases the route
that leads there does. Furthermore, even once the act of faith
has been made, this virtue is such that the object of faith

---

[2] *Catechism of the Catholic Church*, 161.

remains obscure in the sense that we do not see God; we do not see Jesus; we do not see grace at work in the sacraments. We know that faith is grounded on reason, that it is therefore reasonable to believe; we have the certitude that it is true, but still it is not the shadeless brilliance of the beatific vision. Indeed, we see God "now through a glass in a dark manner" (1 Co 13:12) as St Paul explains, that is to say with a certain obscurity. In other words, to have faith is to believe in God without seeing Him, for it is of the essence of faith to give certitude while not removing the merit of believing God on His word.

According to the hypothesis of the final option, however, the soul arriving at death without faith, can then declare itself for God in the full light. From the theory's point of view, it would even seem necessary, in order to choose God, that one see God face to face. What does this mean if not that such a soul would be saved *without* the virtue of faith? If it is precisely the obscurity of faith that gives it to be meritorious of eternal life, how could a choice made in full light be meritorious at all?

The entire faith of the Church and her sacraments are based on the fundamental dogma of the Incarnation. It is because God entered our history and became man that He wanted there to be on earth a lasting sign of His presence, and that presence is the Church and the sacraments. We can say then that, in the eyes of Christianity, salvation consists entirely in meeting Jesus Christ and receiving through Him the forgiveness of sins. Now, according to Catholic Tradition, one meets Christ in this world through sanctifying grace which comes to us especially through the sacraments. One meets Him in the poor and the needy (Mt 25:40); in superiors (cf. Lk 10:16 and Rm 13:1); one meets Him after death in order to be judged. The definitive meeting is in Heaven for those who are judged worthy to enter there (cf. 1 Jn 3:2).

According to Pope St Leo the Great, "what was visible in Christ has passed into the sacraments" so that all generations could have a quasi-physical contact with the Saviour.[3] This is why the Church teaches, following the Lord Himself, the necessity of the sacraments for salvation, in particular that of Baptism ("He that believeth and is baptized shall be saved: but he that believeth not shall be condemned", Mk 16:16),[4] the Eucharist ("Amen, amen, I say unto you: except you eat the flesh of the Son of man and drink his blood, you shall not have life in you", Jn 6:54), and Penance which is the "second plank of salvation" for those who have fallen into mortal sin after Baptism; she also teaches that the sincere desire to receive these sacraments suffices if their actual reception is impossible:

> "If any one saith that the sacraments of the New Law are not necessary unto salvation, but superfluous; and that, without them, or without the desire thereof, men obtain of God, through faith alone, the grace of justification …, let him be anathema."[5]

So when we are told by the final option theorists that there is for all souls an encounter with God at the moment

---

[3] St Leo the Great, *Sermon* 74, 2 : PL 54, 398a: "Quod Redemptoris nostri conspicuum fuit, in sacramenta transivit".

[4] Cf. Council of Trent, *Decree on the Sacraments, on the sacrament of Baptism* can. 5: "If any one saith that baptism is free, that is, not necessary unto salvation; let him be anathema".

[5] Ibid. *On the Sacraments in general*, can. 4.

of death, it would seem to be no exaggeration to affirm that what we have here is nothing less than an alternative to the Church, the sacraments and divine judgment.

Let's take an example that will be readily understood. It used to be customary, and still is among God-fearing souls, to call for a priest when a person is in danger of death, to hear their confession and administer the last rites. How many priests have been dragged out of their beds to go and minister to a dying person in the middle of the night, sometimes at a distance, in bad weather or even in life-threatening circumstances, such as war or contagion? Now, think about it for a moment: what could possibly be the meaning of such heroism should the final option hypothesis reveal itself to be true? If the soul is going to be given the time anyway to see God and make his choice for Him, why bother the poor priest? Granted, many will still want to call the priest to console the dying person, but the fact remains that if the only purpose served by the priest is to offer human consolation, then that function can be performed by lots of people (many of whom would be better suited to the task than the priest...). If the priest is no longer there to bring forgiveness of sins and open the gates to Heaven, if he is no longer the indispensable means of entering into salvific contact with Christ, if he is there only to say some kind and consoling words, there is ultimately no need for him at all and the entire economy of the sacraments collapses.

We could actually push our reasoning a bit further and ask ourselves if the Church herself really serves a purpose. If it is given to everyone to see God at the moment of death, then what's so special about being a Christian, having been baptised and received the Holy Eucharist? It's the very existence of the Church that is compromised by this theory. And this brings us to the question of the necessity of the Church for salvation, which will be mentioned here only in passing.

From the very first centuries of the Christian era, the dogma of salvation as being the unique prerogative of the Catholic Church was consistently put forward by the Fathers and clearly defined by the supreme authority of the Church on several occasions. There can be no doubt that *Outside the Church there is no salvation* is not just a theory that originated in Christian antiquity; it is part and parcel of Catholic dogma. The Fourth Lateran Council, for example, proclaims: "There is one universal Church of the faithful, outside of which no one at all is saved…"[6] The Council of Florence professes:

> This council firmly believes, professes and preaches that none of those outside of the Catholic Church will be partakers of eternal life… unless they are gathered to her before the end.[7]

This teaching is authoritatively restated and further explained by Vatican II:

> Basing itself on Scripture and Tradition, the Council teaches that the Church, a pilgrim now on earth, is necessary for salvation: the one Christ is the mediator and the way of salvation; he is present to us in his body which is the Church. He himself explicitly asserted the necessity of faith and Baptism, and thereby affirmed

---

[6] Council of Lateran IV, *Decree against the Albigensians and the Cathars*, DzH 802.

[7] Council of Florence, Decree of Union *Cantate Domino*, DzH 1351.

at the same time the necessity of the Church which men enter through Baptism as through a door. Hence they could not be saved who, knowing that the Catholic Church was founded as necessary by God through Christ, would refuse either to enter it or to remain in it.[8]

Now, hypotheses such as the final option, for all practical purposes, eliminate the need for the Church, since every single soul would have the exact same opportunity to be saved in an in-death or an after-death experience by which they could choose God and receive sanctifying grace. The understanding here is that obviously, all non-Christians, all non-believers and even all atheists, when they see the love of God face to face, will choose Him. What can "outside the Church there is no salvation" mean in that context? Unless we want to add: "but no one is outside the Church", which makes nonsense of Catholic dogma.

It should no longer be difficult to see that the hypothesis has a hard time finding a place for grace, and in particular for the grace of final perseverance, which is made out to appear almost as a fundamental right of every human being, whatever abuse of the ordinary graces of life they may have been guilty of. In the same way, it becomes difficult to find a place for the doctrine of merit, according to which one draws closer and closer to God through charity and the practice of good works in this life. St Thomas teaches in fact that the body is the necessary instrument of merit: "The source of meriting comes of the soul, while the body is the instrument of the meritorious work."[9] If the moment of

---

[8] Second Vatican Council, Dogmatic Constitution *Lumen Gentium* 14.
[9] St Thomas Aquinas, *Summa Theologiae*, IIIa, q. 49, a. 6, ad 1, The Aquinas Institute for the Study of Sacred Doctrine, 2012, vol. 19, p. 534.

death is the only one that counts definitively, and if one may make at that moment a perfect act of love which propels us into God with all the force of our being, then there is no more room for merits, at least not in the sense that has been defined by the Church:

> If any one saith that the good works of one that is jus-
> tified are in such manner the gifts of God, as that they are
> not also the good merits of him that is justified; or, that
> the said justified, by the good works which he performs
> through the grace of God and the merit of Jesus Christ,
> whose living member he is, does not truly merit increase
> of grace, eternal life, and the attainment of that eternal
> life—if so be, however, that he depart in grace—and also
> an increase of glory; let him be anathema.[10]

Faith and Sacraments are given to us by God Himself. They are the proven way, the "footprints" of God on earth. Let's not take the wrong path, or follow the wrong guide, or mistake God's gems for cheap counterfeit theories which could lead us to lose our dearest possession, our immortal soul. There is one Ark of salvation; let's make sure we're in it, lest we be drowned in the deluge. "Now is the day of salvation" (2 Cor 6:2); the true faith and the sacraments give access to Christ who alone is the Way.

---

[10] Council of Trent, *Decree on Justification,* can. 32.

7

WALKING IN THE SPIRIT

IN A MAGNANIMOUS desire to explain how everybody might make it to Heaven, some writers tell us that it doesn't matter how bad a use one might have made of one's life. At the moment of death one is confronted face to face with God and must make a definitive choice for or against Him, for Heaven or for Hell. In that way, should any soul refuse God, it would be in complete clarity, seeing all the consequences, and accepting them in advance, and this without the unhelpful influence of the passions.

When one weighs carefully the moral consequences of this theory, one discovers that what we are dealing with here is nothing short of a redefinition of mortal sin. This is so because, according to this theory, people who die in what till now was called a state of mortal (that is, deadly) sin cannot be damned unless they commit another mortal sin by rejecting God whose love they see face to face in death. In other words, the mortal sin was not mortal at all, and the only *real* mortal sin is to reject God at death. Consequently, one could commit as many "mortal" sins as one wants during life without going to Hell, for none of them is really mortal. At most, for some authors, "mortal sins" would predispose to making the wrong final option, but they have no real bearings on the eternal destiny of the soul.

This vision of things is contrary to the teaching of the Church, according to which every person is able to commit mortal sin in this life and because of it be separated from God forever. Hear St John Paul II:

> With the whole tradition of the Church, we call mortal sin the act by which man freely and consciously rejects God, His law, the covenant of love that God offers, preferring to turn in on himself or to some created and finite reality, something contrary to the divine will (*conversio ad creaturam*). This can occur in a direct and formal way in the sins of idolatry, apostasy and atheism; or in an equivalent way as in every act of disobedience to God's commandments in a grave matter. Man perceives that this disobedience to God destroys the bond that unites him with his life principle: It is a mortal sin, that is, an act which gravely offends God and ends in turning against man himself with a dark and powerful force of destruction.[1]

This teaching was repeated by the *Catechism of the Catholic Church,* with an insistence on its eternal consequences:

> Mortal sin is a radical possibility of human freedom, as is love itself. It results in the loss of charity and the privation of sanctifying grace, that is, of the state of grace. If it is not redeemed by repentance and God's forgiveness, it causes exclusion from Christ's kingdom

---

[1] St John Paul II, Apostolic Exhortation *Reconciliatio et Poenitentia*, 2 December 1984, no. 17.

and the eternal death of Hell, for our freedom has the power to make choices for ever, with no turning back.[2]

The dire consequences of redefining mortal sin are only too obvious: if the only real mortal sin is to reject God in death, none of the actions of life can have permanent consequences, and so one cannot be held accountable for them; therefore, man is not really responsible for what he does. In stark contrast is the teaching of Sacred Scripture and of the Magisterium of the Church. The book of Sirach (15:13-18), for example, tells us:

> The Lord hateth all abomination of error, and they that fear Him shall not love it. God made man from the beginning, and left him in the hand of his own counsel. He added His commandments and precepts. If thou wilt keep the commandments and perform acceptable fidelity for ever, they shall preserve thee. He hath set water and fire before thee: stretch forth thy hand to which thou wilt. Before man is life and death, good and evil, that which he shall choose shall be given him.

But let's push our reasoning a bit further: if one cannot be held accountable for mortal sin committed in this life, what can this mean other than that man is not really capable of controlling himself? Now this is in complete opposition with the Council of Trent which teaches, following St Augustine, that

> the commandments of God are not impossible to keep, for God does not command impossible things, but

_____

[2] *Catechism of the Catholic Church*, 1861.

when He commands He asks that we do what we can and to pray for what we cannot. He helps us by His grace so that we are able. For "His commandments are not burdensome" (1 Jn 5:3), but "His yoke is sweet and His burden light" (Mt 11:30).[3]

One of the reasons certain authors affirm that people do not really commit mortal sins is their erroneous teaching on the influence of the passions on our free will. It is said that a person who gives himself over to passion no longer has the full use of his reason, and consequently cannot be guilty of a mortal sin. This is an egregious error which denotes the most profound ignorance of the principles of fundamental moral theology. As is often the case with error, it fails to consider the whole of reality. Here, it omits to say that each person remains free to give in to passion or not, as the cited text of the Council of Trent expressly states. Already St Benedict had warned that "death is placed at the very entrance of pleasure."[4] When one hands oneself over to certain passions, they are so vehement that they obscure the intellectual faculty to the point of preventing the will from dominating the senses; but the passage over the threshold—the opening of the heart to passion—*remains voluntary and engages the entire person.*

St Ignatius of Loyola, one of the great saints and mystics of the Church, gives some precious insight into the real meaning of mortal sin, when he invites the retreatant to meditate on the misfortune of a man who went to Hell because of a single mortal sin. He asks us to consider the

---

[3] Council of Trent, *Decree on justification*, c. 12, DzH 1536.
[4] St Benedict of Nursia, *Rule for Monks*, ch. 7, 24-25 ; cf. Sir 18, 30.

just recompense of a soul who, for having acted against the Infinite Goodness is rightly condemned forever.[5] "Acting *against* the Infinite Goodness": that's what mortal sin is, and that's what happens every time one disobeys a commandment of God that contains a serious moral obligation. But why not act *for* and *with* the Infinite Goodness? We have the capacity to do so. If every time we are tempted, instead of giving in to the tempter, we turn to prayer and make a choice for God, we are doing just that, and by the very fact we are choosing God and eternal life with Him.

There is no denying that human beings are subject to various sorts of conditioning (psychosomatic, hereditary, sociological, economic, political...). This has always been and always will be the case. But to seek to absolve all humanity under the pretext of such conditioning manifests very little confidence in what it means to be human in the first place. The Church, basing herself on the teaching of Christ and the efficacy of her sacraments, has confidence that it has been given to man to live in God's grace. She does not, nor can she, resign herself to consider man as a child, victim to his own whims and caprice. Everyone is called to choose between giving of himself and taking for himself. Unfortunately we do see many examples of people choosing the latter, and considering themselves, as it were, as the centre of gravity around which everything else must revolve. Daily choices made for self over others gradually harden the heart and make it impervious to grace. We have no right to justify egotism and sin, but rather the duty to denounce it and call upon those who choose it to convert, to grow up and get out of themselves and their petty little

---

[5] See St Ignatius of Loyola, *Spiritual Exercises*, no. 52.

world. The hard sayings of the Gospel are there to remind us of that. "He that findeth his life, shall lose it: and he that shall lose his life for me, shall find it" (Mt 10:39).

What this suggests then, is that, under the guise of making salvation easy for all, the final option hypothesis actually leads to pessimism as regards the capacity of man to live an upright life that is deserving of salvation. It may be asked if this is not part and parcel of the modern tendency to despair. Having caved in to the widespread pessimism that would have us believe that we are animals who cannot resist the attractions of the passions, the final option theory tries to salvage that despair by giving the hope that, when it's all over, freed at last from the body, one will somehow make the right choice. The true Catholic doctrine, on the contrary, holding man in very high esteem, affirms that he is capable, with the help of Divine Grace, of keeping the commandments, and considers him to be an actor in his own salvation.

The Christian spiritual struggle consists precisely in the effort to overcome temptations, by the good use of grace, as we pray in the Our Father: "lead us not into temptation, but deliver us from evil". The struggle was poignantly described by the Epistle to the Hebrews:

> Therefore we also having so great a cloud of witnesses over our head, laying aside every weight and sin which surrounds us, let us run by patience to the fight proposed to us: looking on Jesus, the author and finisher of faith, who, having joy set before him, endured the cross, despising the shame, and now sitteth on the right hand of the throne of God (Heb 12:1-2).

Pope St John Paul II took issue with the error that man cannot master his passions. He writes:

> Of which man are we speaking? Of man dominated by lust, or of man redeemed by Christ? This is what is at stake: the reality of Christ's redemption. Christ has redeemed us! This means that He has given us the possibility of realizing the entire truth of our being; He has set our freedom free from the domination of concupiscence. And if redeemed man still sins, this is not due to an imperfection of Christ's redemptive act, but to man's will not to avail himself of the grace which flows from that act. God's command is of course proportioned to man's capabilities; but to the capabilities of the man to whom the Holy Spirit has been given; of the man who, though he has fallen into sin, can always obtain pardon and enjoy the presence of the Holy Spirit.[6]

Grace is real; life in the Spirit is real; it transforms us from within. Luther was wrong when he taught that God justifies the sinner from the outside. No, grace truly transforms us from the inside, making us pleasing to God, a "new creature" (Gal 6:15) according to the Heart of God. Let's allow ourselves to be transformed from day to day and never give in to the ambient pessimism about the Christian life. No, we live in the Spirit, and "if we live in the Spirit, let us also walk in the Spirit" (Gal 5:25). And "the fruit of the Spirit is, charity, joy, peace, patience, benignity, goodness, longanimity, mildness, faith, modesty, continency, chastity" (Gal 5:22-23).

---

[6] St John Paul II, *Veritatis Splendor*, 103.

8

EVER ANCIENT, EVER NEW

A<small>T THE PASTORAL</small> level, the apparent divide between the faith and the moral lives of the faithful leads some pastors to orientations that are increasingly irreconcilable with dogma. This is why, having demonstrated that the hypothesis of the final option has no philosophical or theological grounding, we now need to show how pastorally disastrous it can be. For the Catholic, there can be no true pastoral assistance that is not anchored in sound philosophy and in defined dogma, because if this were attempted it would open the door to a dichotomy, a form of spiritual schizophrenia, by which a man would be torn on one side by what he knows from faith and on the other side by what he is living out in practice. The effects of such a theory are of utmost gravity.

It does not seem exaggerated to say that the majority of our Catholic faithful no longer have the strong spiritual drive our ancestors had. If we are to believe the polls, most do not live according to the Church's moral teaching, even when they look up to it as to a lofty ideal; they live, for the most part, like everybody else, even though since the very first generation of Christians, it has always been understood that Christians are different. Why might this be? Could it not possibly be because they no longer have the spiritual incentive of knowing they must be prepared for divine judgment? If they are reassured that "everybody dies and goes to Heaven"—as one is frequently told—, they can only come to the conclusion that there is no risk involved in living as one pleases.

Would it not be precisely in order to preclude such heresy that the Saviour Himself began His preaching with a call to conversion? "Jesus came into Galilee, preaching the gospel of the kingdom of God, and saying: 'The time is accomplished and the kingdom of God is at hand. Repent and believe the gospel'" (Mk 1:14-15). An energetic call to conversion coupled with the unmistakable menace of an everlasting punishment for those who die in mortal sin would become a leitmotif of Jesus' teaching:

> Whosoever shall scandalize one of these little ones that believe in me: it were better for him that a millstone were hanged about his neck and he were cast into the sea. And if thy hand scandalize thee, cut it off: it is better for thee to enter into life, maimed, than having two hands to go into Hell, into unquenchable fire: where their worm dieth not, and the fire is not extinguished. And if thy foot scandalize thee, cut it off: it is better for thee to enter lame into life everlasting than having two feet to be cast into the Hell of unquenchable fire: where their worm dieth not, and the fire is not extinguished. And if thy eye scandalize thee, pluck it out: it is better for thee with one eye to enter into the kingdom of God than having two eyes to be cast into the Hell of fire: where their worm dieth not, and the fire is not extinguished (Mk 9:41-47).

There we have the pastoral approach of Jesus to sinners: the Truth, a Challenge, a Warning. Such is the paradigm for preaching in every age.

When we present death as it is, that is to say, as the day of reckoning and judgment, it is sometimes objected that it sounds like God is lying in ambush for sinners. There is no grounds for this type of presentation. It is false. God finds no pleasure in catching humans unawares at a moment when they are in a state of mortal sin in order to throw them into Hell. This is a blasphemous thought if ever there was one. "Is it my will that a sinner should die, saith the Lord God, and not that he should be converted from his ways, and live?" (Ez 18:23; see also 33:11).

We must not forget that the warning given by Tradition to be ready at every moment does not find its origin in any imaginary sickly anguish with regard to judgment, but *in the Gospel itself*: "Thou fool, this night do they require thy soul of thee" (Lk 12:20), or again: "Wherefore be you also ready, because at what hour you know not the Son of man will come" (Mt 24:44). In reality, death does not put an end to life from the outside. *God is not a passive spectator*; He knows the hour of our death, and He offers each soul His grace: each must respond and be ready. "Behold, I stand at the gate and knock. If any man shall hear my voice and open to me the door, I will come in to him and will sup with him: and he with me" (Ap 3:20).

It is therefore urgent for us to return to a proper understanding of, frequent mention of, and meditation on the four last things: death, judgment, Heaven and Hell. All four are absent today, for even talk of Heaven seems to have disappeared. This is hardly surprising in a materialistic society for which the concept of a transcendental fulfilment is hardly imaginable. Too many Catholics today tend to imagine Heaven as a nice vacation on some olympian beach where the sun will always shine, the water will always be warm and pleasures will be in plenty. They do not seem to know that—in any event they do not live as if—Heaven is the beatific vision of God face to face. That is to say, it is not only being admitted into God's presence, but being introduced into His very life: "We shall see Him as He is" (1 Jn 3:2). Priests need to speak much of Heaven, the true Heaven, where the elect see God face to face, sharing in the immense bliss of all the angels and saints. They need to remind the faithful often that Heaven is not our due, that we have no right to it, that it is infinitely beyond anything we could possibly imagine, and that it is definitely worth giving up a lot for, even suffering and dying for.

Again, it may be objected that the best we can do is speak of the goodness of God and draw people to the faith by avoiding all these topics about sad and harsh realities. This has been in fashion for a number of decades now. When Vatican II in the dogmatic constitution on the Church, *Lumen Gentium,* spoke of the manner in which the grace of salvation might reach those who have not heard of Christ, it added a sentence that seems to have been left aside:

> But often men, deceived by the Evil One, have become vain in their reasonings and have exchanged the truth of God for a lie, serving the creature rather than the Creator. Or some there are who, living and dying in this world without God, are exposed to final despair (*extremae desperationi*).[1]

---

[1] Vatican Council II, Dogmatic Constitution *Lumen Gentium* 16. This

This deception of the devil by which he makes men believe they are on a good path when they are actually on the way to perdition is reminiscent of what Cardinal Journet called the "counter-offensive of the prince of darkness and the city of evil". It is hard not to think of the passage from the book of Proverbs, cited by St Benedict in the Rule: "There is a way which seemeth just to a man: but the ends thereof lead to the deptsh of Hell" (cf. Pr 16:25). If this happens often as Vatican II says—in reality, the Latin text uses the word *saepius*, which does not mean just "often" but "quite often" or "very often" or possibly even, "more often than not"—a question arises: how can we omit to say so? How have we nearly dropped the subject from our repertoire of homilies since this text was promulgated over fifty years ago?

This in turn calls for another question: Is there a correlation between this pastoral approach which insists only on what is positive and good in other religions but refuses to point out their deficiencies, and the decline in conversions and practice of the faith? If there is, it is high time to readjust. A doctor will be all the more attentive to symptoms of disease when he knows it to be frequent. The Congregation for the Doctrine of the Faith did take a step in the right direction when it declared that some prayers and rituals of false religions, "insofar as they depend on superstitions or other errors (cf. 1 Cor 10:20-21), constitute an obstacle to salvation."[2] It is time to take this seriously and to show true pastoral charity to souls, following the words of Paul VI: "It is an outstanding (*praecellens*) man-

---

text is cited in the *Catechism of the Catholic Church*, 844.

[2] Congregation for the Doctrine of the Faith, Declaration *Dominus Iesus*, no. 21, 6 August 2000.

ifestation of charity toward souls to omit nothing from the saving doctrine of Christ". F. D. Bruner writes in the same line of thought:

> When we teach only Jesus' mercies but not his judgments, we disfigure the gospel. If the parables of Judgment are true, then when we skip judgment we are not being loving, as we often think we are.[3]

The unavoidable points of the missionary *kerygma* of all times are summarised by the Princes of the Apostles, St Peter who, on the very day of Pentecost, did not hesitate to challenge the Jews:

> Do penance: and be baptised every one of you in the name of Jesus Christ, for the remission of your sins. And you shall receive the gift of the Holy Ghost.... Save yourselves from this perverse generation (Acts 2:38-40).

St Paul, even in chains and with his life hanging in the balance, made bold to speak to the governor Felix of "justice, continence, and the judgment to come" (Acts 24:25). A theology that would admit a final option in death would make impossible any such serious preaching on these topics. Such a theology waters down the entire moral discourse of the Church, and makes virtually impossible every effort towards a reform of morals.

Already St Augustine had realised this when debating with those who seek to establish that, in spite of the repeated

---

[3] F. D. Bruner *Matthew, A commentary,* Eerdmans, 2004, p. 550.

warnings of Sacred Scripture, all will be saved. Augustine wrote that, when arguing for the salvation of all, including those who refuse to convert,

> they are pleading their own cause, promising themselves a delusive impunity for their own disreputable lives by supposing an all-embracing mercy of God towards the human race.... It is *excessively presumptuous* to assert that there will be eternal punishment for none of those who, so God has said, will go to punishment which will be eternal...

And to give the ultimate reason for this: "Anybody who has not been transferred to the side of Christ *while he lives in the body* is thereafter reckoned as belonging to the Devil's party..."[4]

The late Monsignor James O'Connor had this profound insight to offer concerning St Augustine's approach to these questions:

> [Saint] Augustine admired the merciful intent of those who think that we may truly hope for the salvation of all human beings, but as teacher and pastor he rejected the opinion as well as its consequences. Indeed, pastorally speaking, it could prove to be, as he saw, a deceptive mercy, one that would lead to a presumption of salvation for all and end by abetting the damnation of many. [...] It is such a sober awareness that the words of

---

[4] St Augustine, *City of God*, Book 21, ch. 18 and 24; trans. Henry Bettenson, emphasis added.

Jesus and the teaching of the Church would appear to inculcate, and better guides in this matter we cannot have.[5]

Indeed, no other guides do we have. The teaching of Christ, relayed to us by the Church, is our *only* guide. It is ever solid, for it is ever old, but it is ever new as well, for it alone has eternal youth and leads to true freedom in the Spirit. "You shall know the truth: and the truth shall make you free" (Jn 8:32).

---

[5] J. T. O'Connor, *Land of the Living : a Theology of the Last Things*, Catholic Book Publishing, 1992, p. 82-83.

9

ARS MORIENDI

IT SOMETIMES HAPPENS that one runs across an unhealthy fixation on death. In our day, however, there seems to be more of a concerted effort to play down and hide death; everything is done to make it seem insignificant. Between these two extremes, there is place for a serene contemplation of death which, far from being sickly, can contribute to a happy life. If one desires to die well, one must live well, and if one desires to live well, one must make the effort to think that one day we must die.

> A good name is better than precious ointments: and the day of death than the day of one's birth. It is better to go to the house of mourning, than to the house of feasting: for in that we are put in mind of the end of all, and the living thinketh what is to come (Ecc 7:2-3).

Truth be told, meditation on death is not a Christian invention. The ancient philosophers were fond of encouraging their disciples to think of death. It suffices to recall the strong words of Plato in *Phaedo*. For example, Socrates says to Crito:

> I want to make my argument before you, my judges, as to why I think that a man who has truly spent his

life in philosophy is probably right to be of good cheer in the face of death and to be very hopeful that after death he will attain the greatest blessings yonder… I am afraid that other people do not realize that the one aim of those who practice philosophy in the proper manner is to practice for dying and death.[1]

In our days too, moral philosophy will do well to meditate on death. Such meditation is, in reality a meditation on life, in the sense that a good philosophy of life teaches its adepts to die to the images and seductions of façades and appearances in order to reach, thanks to anticipated "death to self" the authentic life which knows not the vicissitudes and contingencies of bodily life. This is so true that, in one sense, to live is to die, and in another, to die is to live. The thought of death helps us to be detached from the illusions of an existence centred on *having* in order to fix our attention on the only ultimate reality, that of *being*. If this meditation behooves philosophers, and allows them to live a happier life on earth, how much more is it becoming for Christians who know that beyond the gates of death there lies an unending blissful life of communion with God or an awful existence of separation from Him?

It is no surprise then that many Christian authors have excelled in the *ars bene moriendi*—the art of dying well. There is a vast current of spirituality which prescribes to hold these great truths continually before one's eyes. St Benedict engraves in the heart of his disciples: "Fear the day of judgment. Dread Hell. Desire eternal life with all spiritual

---

[1] *Phaedo*, IX, 63-64.

ardour. Have death each day before one's eyes."[2] The saint summarises here a long tradition from which he had only to draw in order to provide such crucial considerations for his monks and for all Christians. Following the monastic tradition, the author of the *Imitation of Christ* conveys to us some most incisive ponderings:

> If thou hadst a good conscience thou wouldst not much fear death. It were better for thee to fly sin than to be afraid of death. If thou art not prepared today, how shalt thou be tomorrow? Tomorrow is an uncertain day; and how dost thou know that thou shalt be alive tomorrow?... Strive now so to live that in the hour of thy death thou mayst rather rejoice than fear. Learn now to die to the world that then thou mayst begin to live with Christ. Learn now to despise all things that then thou mayst freely go to Christ. Chastise thy body now by penance that thou mayst then have an assured confidence.[3]

In this way, it can be seen that the *ars bene moriendi* consists above all in the *ars bene vivendi*—the art of living well. This spirituality is proven; it is solid and serious; without being morbid, it fills the heart with fear that is both advantageous and reverent before the holiness of God. Yes, the thought of death inspires fear, but fear that comes naturally to frail man in this life and that protects him, such as the fear of snakes or wild animals; it also inspires him to consider

---

[2] S. Benedict of Nursia, *Rule for Monks*, ch. 4, 44-47, trans. Justin McCann.

[3] *Imitation of Christ*, B. 1, ch. 23.

seriously what awaits him after death. Such fear, properly
understood, can only make for a happier and more peaceful
life. Certainly, as John Paul II reminds us, "the meditation
on death goes hand in hand with meditation on sin, because
death, according to the words of Divine Revelation, entered
the world because of sin (cf. Rm 5:12)."[4] Or again: "Man
fears death as he fears what will come after death. He fears
judgment and punishment, and this fear is salvific: it must
not be erased from man."[5] But this salutary fear preserves
from much greater and graver fears. St John Henry Newman
puts these words in the mouth of the angel addressing the
truly Christian soul as it enters eternity:

> *"It is because*
> *Then thou didst fear, that now thou dost not fear.*
> *Thou hast forestalled the agony, and so*
> *For thee the bitterness of death is past."*[6]

In the traditional Litany of the Saints we find this invocation: *A subitanea et improvisa morte, libera nos, Domine (From
a sudden and unprovided death, deliver us, O Lord)*. To be
taken away abruptly without being able to prepare oneself
for death, appears as a danger from which we want to be
protected. But if, as the final option theory teaches, there
is no such thing as a sudden death, for death always occurs
with full consciousness, the invocation makes no sense. If
people pray to be delivered from a sudden death, it can only
be out of fear of not having the time to prepare themselves
for death and judgment. If death, however, opens the gate
to the full consciousness of self and allows a definitive choice,

---

[4] St John Paul II, *Homily* of 1 November 1987.
[5] St John Paul II, *Homily* of 23 April 1995.
[6] St J. H. Newman, *The Dream of Gerontius*.

not only should one not fear that it be sudden, but it is better that it be so, for in this way one avoids the pains of the agony with the possibility of revolt against God due to the sufferings one endures. There seems to be no exaggeration in saying that the final option hypothesis opens the door to euthanasia.

There was a time, and it is not far past, when the Church took great care not to give the impression that one could be saved in any condition. This is why Christian burial is still refused—or should be—to those who have died in an attitude of open hostility towards the Church or even only separated from her without giving any sign of conversion before death (cf. Canon 1184). In our day, the insistence on the primacy of individual conscience has led to give less importance to the example that each person gives to others by his life, and from there to accept practices in themselves scandalous. Hope and even presumption in favour of subjective sincerity have taken precedence over objective and public profession of the faith; "sincerity" has become the supreme criterion for the evaluation of a moral and spiritual life. If all that really matters is subjective sincerity, faith and its demands no longer mean anything.

And this brings us to yet another consideration. The hypothesis appears to be optimistic about death, but if we examine the matter closely, we perceive that it is rather quite depressing. It leads us to believe that in this life one cannot attain happiness by living a virtuous life, because one is conditioned by the passions and therefore deprived of true freedom; one has to wait for death in order to become the person of one's dreams. Having discarded the perspective of eternal sanctions for the failings accomplished in time, this hypothesis sanctions the rejection of all responsibility and leads straight to the collapse of Christian morals and indeed of human morality itself. It is of the utmost importance that man remind himself that he is a creature on earth, that God is in Heaven, and that man's eternal destiny depends upon the merciful bounty of God on which one may not count rashly. To presume on God's mercy is a grave sin. "Be not deceived, God is not mocked. For what things a man shall sow, those also shall he reap" (Gal 6:7-8).

When one has taken the full measure of what it means to die and be judged, one can no longer understand the mindlessness involved in putting off the time of preparation. The hour of death must be anticipated, prepared for by prayer, examination of conscience, confession. Of course, God can give exceptional graces at the approach of death, and there are indeed many stories of souls who were salvaged at the last moment thanks to the prayers and good example of others, or perhaps thanks to a good habit of prayer or a good work that they performed during their life. But it is gravely presumptuous to count on such a grace.

That is why the saints were so determined to sting the consciences of sinners and plead with them not to put off their reconciliation with God to a hypothetical day which may never come, or to the hour of death which, as St Alphonsus de Liguori tells us, far from being a favourable time to set the record straight, is actually a time of great trouble and confusion in which the mind is darkened and the will is weakened. If one has not the strength to examine one's conscience and confess one's sins when in good health, how can one have it when in the throes of death, when illness and lassitude make every effort a torture? After quoting the Lord's words in Lk 12:40 ("Be you then also ready: for at what hour you think not the Son of man will come"),

St Alphonsus—who, it is good to recall, is a doctor of the Church and patron saint of moral theologians and confessors—points out that the Lord does not tell us to prepare when death arrives, but to be ready at all times for that hour; this is essentially because the time of death is a time of trouble in which it is nearly impossible to prepare well to appear before the judge and obtain a favourable sentence...[7]

To become masters in the art of dying we must become masters in the art of living. We have but one life and one death. Let's make them beautiful for God.

---

[7] See St Alphonsus de Liguori, *Preparation for Death*, ch. 9 and *Way of Salvation*, ch. 10.

ETERNITY BEGINS NOW

M Y MOTHER HAD died. As I journeyed home, the under-takers removed her mortal remains from the family home to the funeral home until visitation the day before the funeral: eight full days during which her body was absent, as if she had never lived among us. I had to make arrangements with the funeral home to come and pray each day, as generations of Christians had done in their homes, before the mortal remains of the cherished woman who had given me life.

This personal experience is indicative of what I would like to stress in these concluding thoughts. Our world has removed death from the horizon, pushed it aside, trying to pretend that it does not exist, that it is, really, nothing at all. In the ages of Christendom, and even far beyond among the great philosophers of ancient Greece, contemplation of and preparation for death was an essential part of a good life. But there is a difference—the ancient philosophers did not have the revelation that we do; for us it takes on an entirely new meaning: preparing for death is making ready for judgment and disposing oneself to be worthy of eternal life in Heaven as opposed to being lost forever in Hell. That is why the death of a loved one is so important for a family, and why it is a very special time of prayer for all, young and old, who are confronted and can see death face to face, and understand that they too need to prepare for it.

Now we can understand why the saints encouraged meditation on death. The old Roman liturgy gives the example of Saint Sylvester who, as the oration for his feast tells us (26 November in the traditional Roman Missal), meditated on the vanity of this world before an open grave. We already saw that St Benedict admonishes his monks to "fear the day of judgment, dread Hell, desire eternal life with all spiritual longing, keep death daily before one's eyes."[1] Such contemplation of death has nothing at all in common with a morbid outlook on life. On the contrary, the true Christian looks forward to death as the longed-for encounter with God whom he has loved and served; his fear of death is transformed into a saving fear whose prod is love, and he is on that account able to see it approach peacefully, knowing that the moment of the definitive encounter with the Beloved is now at hand. The objection according to which the Church in the old days would have been responsible for making people's lives miserable by its insistence on death and judgment is not only groundless, but can actually be turned back on the accusers, for in our day and age where eternal life is no longer part of the horizon, people live as if this life were everything, and they are none the more happy and fulfilled. On the contrary, psychosomatic illnesses, depression and suicide are at never-before-seen highs.

It would even seem that it is precisely the fact that the eschatological horizon has been obscured that modern man is prey to such depression. If this life is all there is, then we are, at best, sophisticated animals trying to make for ourselves

---

[1] See *Rule of St Benedict*, ch. 4.

a relatively comfortable existence, rarely succeeding, often failing lamentably. But if we know that we are on a journey towards eternity and that at death an unending life shall be opened for us, the perspective changes entirely.

So it is certain that we can speak of this life as being an eschatological commencement, the beginning of the eternal realities ahead. Here below we see through a glass, in obscurity (cf. 1 Cor 13:12), but through faith we know with absolute certitude that beyond the veil there is God. Such a vision of things radically changes the way we look at life, for it helps us give each moment an intensity it could not possibly have otherwise. When it dawns on us that our salvation is not something to be obtained perilously at the last moment, but something that is achieved here and now by the choices we make, then our outlook changes. We know that if we choose to love and serve God and neighbour here and now, our actions have an eternal weight of glory (cf. 2 Cor 4:17). We know, thanks to faith, that we are already, in a way, in eternal life, for the Lord Himself, especially in St John's Gospel (cf. Jn 3:36; 5:24; 6:47, 55), tells us that if we believe in Him, we *have* eternal life, already here and now.

Such are the thoughts that made Christianity a revolution in a pagan world 2,000 years ago. Such are the awesome thoughts that led the martyrs to their torture singing the praises of God. Such are the sublime thoughts that peopled the deserts and the cloisters with men and women determined to give every moment of their brief life to God, loved above all things. Such are the noble thoughts that are at the beginning of so many works of Christian charity to the poor, the needy, the crippled, the blind, the lepers, etc. And such are the thoughts that have inspired Christian parents to accept all the children God wants to give them and rear them in His love—often at such great cost to themselves—so that they too may become saints in glory. Eternity begins now, today; at this very moment I can win my Heaven, and you can win yours.

When this comes home to us, the cause of the sadness of the modern world is revealed, and we begin to see that this omnipresent gloom is for having lost the innocence of the virtue that was brought to it by faith in a Man who was God, and who spent His life on earth teaching us the way to Heaven, for He knew better than anyone that this life is short, and that it has no meaning whatsoever if it does not lead to a blessed eternity.

As we bring these pages to a close, we need only draw the conclusion which the hypothesis of a final option seems to hide, namely, the importance of the historical time of our life in this world. If the definitive option—the only one which really counts—takes place outside of time, and especially if it is impossible that it take place in time due to the attractions of concupiscence and the pressure of multiple influences, then how can one continue to give true value to what happens in time? Misguided insistence on the moment of death as being the moment of choice abets the grave error of creating a dichotomy between the present life and eternal life.

In reality, earthly life prepares eternal life, each of its instants being a possible moment of eternity, in the sense that we choose our destiny through concrete acts; our daily actions either orient us toward God or separate us from Him; one can, under the influence of grace, turn oneself toward the Infinite Good, but one can also resist grace and turn toward the creature, preferring it to the Creator, and by the very fact, rejecting eternal love. Knowing that at each moment one can die and appear before the tribunal of Christ to receive either an eternal reward or an unending punishment is a mighty stimulant to living an upright life and sacrificing oneself for one's brothers and sisters, especially when charity has not attained a degree of sufficient intensity to act out of pure love. In this sense, we can say that eternity begins now, and if it is not prepared for now, there is no guarantee whatsoever that there will be time later. This supposes asceticism, for one must die each day to oneself and one's vices, according to the word of St Paul "I die daily" (1 Cor 15:31).

This is where we meet with one of the paradoxes of the Christian faith: at each moment the Christian prepares for death, for he knows that Christ can appear at any moment. However, far from feeling anguish due to the imminence of the end, this certitude gives him—or should give him at least if he truly lives his faith—an unchanging peace and calm amidst both interior and exterior struggles, which allow him to develop a quality of life unknown to those who do not have faith in eternal life. We can remind ourselves here of the countless achievements of the era of medieval Christianity which still provoke the admiration of all, or the masterpieces produced by men who professed to die to the world, or again the radiant joy on the faces of souls who have given all to the service of the poor out of love for God. Thus one can see that living for God not only gives unshakeable confidence that at the moment of death one will receive a merciful judgment, but also allows one to live with greater fullness each moment of life.

If it is true that we have only one life and that we will be definitively judged at the moment of death according to the way we lived it, it is also true that the encounter with Christ is not just a future event reserved to the moment of death. It is here and now that salvation begins. It is today that Christ speaks to us and seeks to win our heart.

Each time we recite the Ave Maria, we ask the Virgin to pray for us "now and at the hour of our death". At each recitation, the "now" and the "hour of our death" draw closer. They have never been closer than they are today. What we must never forget is that the only adequate preparation for *that* hour is *this* hour: it is the *nunc*, the "now", it is each of the moments in which we are given to live in fidelity to the grace of God and in service to our neighbour. If time, as long as it is, has no proportion with eternity,—"For I reckon that the sufferings of this time are not worthy to be compared with the glory to come that shall be revealed in us" (Rm 8:18)—each moment can be lived in relation with it, for at each moment our choices give shape to who we are and make us who we will be for all eternity. In this sense, we can say that at each moment of our life carries with it eternal value.

Eternity will soon be here: the night of death is coming, when no one can work. Therefore, let us work now, *whilst it is day* (Jn 9:4).

CPSIA information can be obtained
at www.ICGtesting.com
Printed in the USA
FSHW011301150121
77731FS

9 780648 868859